AMERICA 51

ALSO BY COREY TAYLOR

Seven Deadly Sins (2012)

A Funny Thing Happened on the Way to Heaven (2013)

You're Making Me Hate You (2015)

AMERICA 51

A PROBE INTO THE REALITIES THAT ARE HIDING INSIDE "THE GREATEST COUNTRY IN THE WORLD"

COREY TAYLOR

Da Capo Press

Da Capo Press
Hachette Book Group
1290 Avenue of the Americas, New York, NY 10104
www.dacapopress.com
@DaCapoPress; @DaCapoPR

Printed in the United States of America
First Edition: August 2017
Published by Da Capo Press, an imprint of Perseus Books, LLC, a subsidiary of Hachette Book Group, Inc.

Print book interior design by Jane Raese
Set in 10-point Utopia
Editorial production by Christine Marra, *Marra*thon Editorial Production Services, www.marrathoneditorial.org

Library of Congress Cataloging-in-Publication Data has been applied for.
ISBN 978-0-306-82544-6 (hardcover)
ISBN 978-0-306-82545-3 (ebook)

LSC-C
10 9 8 7 6 5 4 3 2 1

CONTENTS

As always, to my family, my friends . . .

and most of all, to my children:

Griffin, Ryan, Angie, Haven, Lawson, Aravis

This world will be yours later.

I'll try to pick up a bit before I close for the night.

Love you all.

All that is necessary for the triumph of evil is
that good men (and women) do NOTHING.

—EDMUND BURKE (paraphrased)

Power corrupts.
And Absolute Power corrupts absolutely.

—LORD ACTON

When they kick at your front door
How you gonna come?
With your hands on your head
Or on the trigger of your gun?

—THE CLASH, "The Guns of Brixton"

America . . . what if God doesn't care?

—SLIPKNOT, "Gematria (The Killing Name)"

CHAPTER 1

ON THE ROAD, REVISITED

SO.

Sooooooo . . .

Here's a funny story that isn't funny at all.

Two political parties walk into a bar. One gets shitfaced hammered and nominates a loud, crude, egotistical, childish, bullying (yet easily butt-hurt) jackass cunt of an orange billionaire to be the president of the United States of America. The other, equally smug and unapproachable, decides to abstain from such low-quality behavior and spends the entire time reminding you that not only are they special because they're not at *all* like the other candidate but also that they need you to love them for *little more* than that reason alone or else they will look down on you with piteous disdain and appallingly bitter bemusement. Both sides had their fair share of intelligent detractors as well as their equal legions of completely devoted zealots. Most people in the middle were left with a terrible choice to make: vote for someone you didn't *really* support, thus wiping your ass with your constitutional rights as a citizen, or choose someone that nobody else was going to vote for and cast your vote that way, realizing the same result yet feeling a little better about yourself. That is exactly what a lot of people did.

Granted, a lot of people genuinely supported the various candidates. Trump had his swamp-draining pussy grabbers, Hillary had the "I'm With Her" folk, and all the holier-than-thou angsty coffee drinkers had Stein and Johnson, vowing to take their toys and go home because Bernie wasn't allowed to come out and play. Sheisty shit was going on all over the place, and it looked like there was absolutely no way the situation could get worse. Then we watched, in incredulous horror, as that same orange prick, the one who'd openly mocked *so* many others, won the Electoral College, even as he lost the popular vote by nearly 3 million votes. I couldn't believe my fucking eyes: DONALD FUCKING TRUMP WAS GOING TO BE PRESIDENT OF THE UNITED STATES OF AMERICA. Writing it here and now, it *still* doesn't feel very real. Reading that sentence back, I have to keep stopping myself from correcting it. It's true: Donald Trump is the president.

He ain't *my* fucking president. But he is *the* president, and we'll leave it at that.

I'll bet boners to nipple clamps that I was just like most of you: glued to CNN in pure dread as Trump's numbers kept getting higher and higher. So many people were texting me, saying, "Is this *really* happening? What the shit?!" I kept myself from losing it by calming *them* down, saying, "Don't worry! It's still early. It'll be *fine*! Our country can't be *that* fucking stupid!" Then, by the time Pennsylvania fell, I sat stunned on my sofa, realizing that my country was in fact *that* fucking stupid. I whispered a quote from the original *Planet of the Apes*, when Chuck Heston sees Lady Liberty up to her tits in the sand and shouts, "You maniacs! Damn you! Damn you *all* to Hell!"

This book started out *very* different.

It started out with a disclaimer about the dangers of foisting a despot like Donald Drumpf (real family name) on this country. It talked about a Hillary victory I was so sure was going to happen. I wasn't really that invested in her per se—I just didn't want the Cheeto to win. I had faith that it wouldn't happen, that most blue-collar people would come to their senses and go the other way. But that never happened—and in fact, it got worse. The GOP, otherwise known as the Republicans, ended up keeping their majority in the Senate and doubling down on their super-majority in the House of Representatives, paving the way for a *whole* lot of bad defunding to go down. So the presidency and Congress are held by the Republicans, while the Supreme Court—the other third of our three tiers of government—was stuck at eight members because Congress refused to allow Barack Obama to nominate a new judge. Let's hear it for Gorsuch, ladies and gentlemen . . .

This book started out with some hope that after a Trump scare, the Democrats could reach over and take some of these working-class folks—*my* folks—and show them that they are in fact *their* political party. It started out with a vision of seeing the GOP eat a lot of crow for tying their carts to a chauvinistic cocksucker afraid of his own shadow who is easily goaded into saying something pathetic. It had a lot of instances where it would show the GOP for the hypocrites they are: purporting to be for smaller government and yet digging their fingers into just as many programs, grants, and rights as the Democrats do. I wanted to break this shit down like a DJ after a wedding for you all. Then he *won*. He fucking won. No matter what he'd said or done, no matter how vile and fucked up he was or was *going* to be, no matter how much he'd lied and lied and lied and fucking lied . . . he'd won.

In the big game at the political table, he'd played his Trump card and beat the house, setting it back a few points, to be sure.

When that happened I walked over to the computer on which I write my books, opened up all the chapters I had already started on, highlighted hours' worth of words, work, and effort . . . and deleted it all. Highlight. Delete. Start again. It *hurt.* I was tied up in fucking knots for days, simultaneously catching shit for not doing enough to get the vote out and also ducking flying turds for *daring* to insinuate that because Trump had won, there would be an outbreak of violence against blacks, Latinos, Muslims, the entire LGBT-plus community, women, and so on. I was harassed for "instigating the violence by suggesting that violence might happen"—which, it correctly turned out, happened whether I'd said anything or not. Swastikas were spray painted on churches and mosques across the country. People were attacked in earnest. Angry white men shouted their contempt for anyone who had the audacity to be neither white nor male on flights and on subway cars. I can say this because there are videos of this happening. There are videos, and NO ONE WAS ARRESTED OR TAKEN TO FUCKING TASK OVER IT. No punishments for obscenity or vocal hate—just wanded, waived, and sent on their way. It lasted for a while, even as the protests mounted and the Trump supporters became just as "snowflake" and "triggered" as the liberals they loved to hate. Time to tuck in and settle down to wait for what was next.

But here's the thing, and you're going to think I'm *fucking* crazy right now: I'm GLAD he won. HOLD YOUR FUCKING HORSES, YOU MOTHERFUCKERS! Before some of you angry lefty pricks start bombarding me with crazy spam and dizzying examples of why the Trump Effect is going to burn this nation into cinders, then piss on those cinders, then stuff those cinders up Melania's bleached asshole, then grunt those same filthy ashes into a champagne glass, *then* have those poopy, champagne-ridden, pissy American ashes blown straight up into his own privileged asshole live on C-Span . . . Jesus, sorry about that folks. I really got off on a riff there, Sonny Rollins style. I don't even remember where the hell I was going with all of that. Was I going to talk about the new First Lady's nudes? Was I going to talk about those uncomfortable moments between Donald and Ivanka? By the way that whole pissy ashes metaphor takes on a whole new meaning given the "Golden Gate" controversy—oh, Donald . . .

Anyway, before *any* of that absolutely happens—and there are great chances that it will—let me explain that sentiment. I'm not happy that this election has divided our country into gnarly tribes of discontent. I'm not happy that some people are scared and others think it is fair game to terrorize. I'm not happy that the protests seem to go on and on because they just keep looking for new reasons to be upset. I'm happy because it set my record straight, sharpened my gaze, and put me back on the path. Check it out.

Yes, Donald Trump is the president (at least for now)—NOT MY PRESIDENT, but The President. That's not to say that I'll be happy when the Right tries to take out the various programs that are helping people, like it or not, get through their life. I won't keep quiet when they add to the deficit because they don't have any answers better than what is already there, but they won't admit to it. I also won't stand by as they try to "scale back" the powers of those who oppose them, like the intelligence communities, the "checks and balances" parts of our governments . . . or the American voting population. If they want a revolution, they'll fucking get one because they suck at math: WAY MORE PEOPLE VOTED AGAINST TRUMP THAN VOTED FOR HIM, AND HE'D

BETTER FUCKING REMEMBER THAT. The Orange Mandate does not exist.

No, I'm glad for different reasons—two reasons, to be exact: because up to that point, this book was a piece of shit, and to be quite honest, so is our two-party system. This book was really just me ranting and raving about how right I was about Trump and the Right and all that shit blah blah blah fucking GET OVER YOURSELF TAYLOR. I was acting exactly like the political party I *thought* I supported, until I realized that was the very reason that people found it so hard to support that party—not only could they not relate to it, but they felt judged and belittled for not coming off as a shiny shell from the intelligentsia. More down-to-earth people were siding with an egomaniacal Cheeto than they were a candidate that should have smoked him like a throw-away gang member in *Death Wish 2*.

They were tired of walking into vocabulary traps, akin to getting a face full of spider webs carrying laundry to the washer in the basement. Can't say this, can't say that . . . it's ridiculous. You can't say "god bless you"—it has to be just plain ol' "bless you." You can't say certain pronouns anymore—you end up sounding like a possessed Speak & Spell when the batteries are getting low. From "Merry Christmas" to "motherfucker," it's become quite a lesson in pomposity. That leads to what we'll talk about later: adverse empathy. English writer extraordinaire W. S. Gilbert said, "When everyone is somebody, then no one's anybody." I'll paraphrase a bit for this case: when everything's offensive, then nothing will be.

As much as pundits and pollsters would love to paint the two parties in broader terms, these politicians had become people you couldn't identify with, for better or for worse. Personally, I don't think you should want that in a politician, but then again

I think most pols are preening shit talkers with two faces and too many pockets. In Trump, at least most of us could see the idiot reflected back on us. I never had that with Hillary; to be honest, I think most Americans thought she was so busy judging them that they never took the time to listen to what she was saying. I'm not going to drag you all through that bastard election again—I'm fairly certain it added years to us all. My point is this—most of us, most of the people on the street just trying to make a living, don't want a president who makes us feel like shit about ourselves. Like it or not, wrong or right, I believe people had that feeling about Hillary—and to be honest, about almost *all* Democrats, really. People don't like being beat over the head with how much smarter you are than they are. I'm not saying that was the *whole* factor, but it's definitely why most people found it easier to vote for someone else.

Like I said, I have leaned Democrat for years. However, I'm giving serious thought to going full Independent, merely because I feel the same way a lot of people do—judged by the upper crust, and I'm talking about *both* parties now. Republicans hide a little better behind their guns and their God, and no pun intended but God forbid you be a little outside the box. Sure, they *want* you to feel at home in their party—they're the "Party of the People"! But you have to be *their* kind of people. If not, they'll take away your rights quicker than you can say "Pro-Choice." The Dems are just as bad. One of the biggest problems with the Democrats is they're savvy enough to embrace cutting edge liberties like abortion or transgender identities, and yet they cannot comprehend why some people have such a hard time coming to grips with that, especially people with a deep background in faith. To regular folks, these are concepts that are as foreign as speaking French to a kindergartener from Topeka. They've never even thought about the notion before, but now they feel like they're being *forced* to deal with it, *forced* to support it, *forced* to just accept it, even though they're not really sure if they truly understand it.

No one explains anything anymore—they just blurt out shit like they do on Twitter or Facebook or in any of the comments sections where good grace and common sense go to die. It's ratcheting up the narcissism at an alarming rate. But we don't really communicate anymore anyway. We go out of our way to make slamming statements and dare a motherfucker to say anything that deigns to be contradictory and then we retaliate with pure digital venom and righteousness. Abandon all hope, ye who log on here. So it's no wonder that anyone regarded as intelligent is regarded as an "elite libtard SJW" and anyone regarded as working class, maybe a little simpler in their approach to life, nothing more, is regarded as a "white trash racist redneck." A population marginalized before they can ever have a conversation is going to do incredible things . . . like nominate and elect Donald Trump.

So this book went from being a sanctimonious editorial on how much I think I know about what's right for you in my own head and the shitty sauces held within, to a book that will now take a deeper look at what the hell is really going on, and I mean with *all of it*: the political parties, who they say they stand for, who they *really* stand for, who the people think stand for them, where all of this is going, where I hope we land, and a subtle little history lesson on politics in this country. Plus, I want to walk you through some of the cooler pieces of real estate here in these United States, stuff that maybe you forgot about, stuff that maybe you didn't know about, places and people to tickle the fancy and engage a bit of nostalgia or—hold your ass—real patriotism, not that shit that the government tries to shill on late night television. This is more about looking under the bed for toys we always forget we have but would love to play with and cherishing that joy of rediscovery before the clamps of cynicism come rushing back to remind us of real life and the grim reality of paying bills and doing laundry . . . you know, REAL-LIFE SHIT.

You see the thing that bothers me about a lot of these politicians is that we only see them on TV. We only see them in the papers. We don't know them. "Just like you . . ." Motherfucker, *please*. When was the last time you missed a bill and spent a week or two freaking out about it? When was the last time you only got a few hours of sleep because you got young kids and if *they* don't sleep, neither do *you*? When was the last time you had to choose between food for your kids or the electric bill? Did you *ever* have to go through that kind of *real* shit? If you did, show me some photos. Let's see some video. Let's hear how you'd make a sandwich if you didn't have anything to make a sandwich *with*, asshole. Me? I remember all that shit. It's the blessing and the curse of having an active mind. I remember sleeping in closets, bathtubs, on the street, in the same clothes for days because we had no money for anything. If you gave me one piece of bread right now and sent me into a kitchen bereft of anything that resembles "sandwich fixins'" I would walk out with a fucking sandwich. And I'd eat that fucker because I know what it means to be broke and desperate. I know what it means to have that sinking feeling in your gut that you might not get the rent in but there will be dinner for that next week. I'd like proof to see if Paul Ryan could come up with some shit like that before he thought about voting to gut programs like Medicare, Social Security, the ACA and certain types of welfare.

But that's not saying that anyone should be prejudged because they've done well for themselves or because they have an education either. You work your ass off, you should be allowed to enjoy it—but don't forget where you come from, and don't make motherfuckers feel like you're rubbing it in. Herein lies the problem, and we finally come to the revelation that changed this book completely. This book is less about politics, and more about . . . us. We, the People, standing like schlock jocks at a Halloween weenie roast, waiting to give out prizes for "best shitty Crow costume," we have become the very reason for our downfall. The country's a mess because *we* are a collection of fucking messes. Our politicians are overwhelmingly fucked because *we* are overwhelmingly fucked, and I mean IN THE ASS, NO SPIT, NO LUBE fucked. We don't talk *to* each other anymore, face to face, like civilized human beings. We scream AT each other, constantly, violently, anonymously, from behind computer screens and cell phones, in an almost perpetual duel of "I have to be right." Do you know why this country is starting to eat itself? It's because we handed it a knife and fork, and said "Chow down, Cupcake."

We have no accountability for anyone anymore, because we refuse to accept it ourselves. We have no boundaries for right or wrong *or* fancy and common sense. Who's going to listen if you're constantly butting your heads together? Who's going to care if someone's hurting or needs help if the only thought that goes through our heads is "Well, they should've helped themselves. . ." or "Nobody helped ME when I was in trouble, so . . ." These are fucking cop-outs in the face of the reality that it takes a whole lot of energy these days to be a good person, or at least that's the way people would make it seem anyway, as so many people are wearing themselves out patting themselves on the back. Let me ask you this: when, in our history, did the concepts of "the welfare of the people" and "fiscal responsibility" become mutually exclusive? Hmm? Can *anyone* answer that for me? I'll tell you right now what it's all about, and this is exactly why there will be *no* draining of any swamps or construction on any fancy walls or incarceration for political adversaries, much to the chagrin of the howling cunts who voted for the Cheeto: because behind closed doors, with the lights low, they're just as despicable as the ones across the aisle they all purport to hate. They are the mirrors on the bridge at Gitmo, the sentries keeping stride between the Koreas: they are exactly what you fear, Trump included.

We've also become a gigantic tribe of total hypocrites. We talk shit about each other's flaws when our own back stories have enough plot holes to drive convoys of semis through, nonstop twenty-four hours a day. The Right keeps telling the Left to "get over it" and "you didn't see *us* protesting when Obama won"—when there is in fact clear video, audio, and photographic *proof* of these people protesting when Obama won, for the better part of eight years. The Left keeps harping and harping on offensive language and yet has *no* problems whatsoever with labeling someone a Nazi or a bigot or a racist if it seems like they're not winning the argument—"you know, like I'm *supposed to*!" This kind of behavior stems from years of resentment and yet has festered and come to fruition under the Miracle-Gro speed of tech and social media.

I'd love to sit here and write about some of the heroes fighting for us on the other side of the fence, but I just can't do that because, like you all, I've lost a lot of faith in our "leaders." Our governing bodies are running out of compatible tissues. Every generation of politicians gets more extreme, leaving behind the concerns of the populace in favor of a narrower, more personal agenda. They don't want to end the ACA because it hurts the American people; they want to end the ACA because they're vindictive crab catchers who are still pissed off that *their* version of the ACA didn't get passed in the first place. This is less about *you* and more about *them,* and it's getting to the point where I can see it's been like that for a long time. Idealism is now a dirty word. Those fuckers in DC know better than anyone that we're all in different books on different pages, and they exploit it: Why do you think no one gets held accountable? Why do you think a bastard with more strikes against him became president? The reasons are in our differences.

This is where that stops, and I mean RIGHT FUCKING NOW.

I will *not* stand by while zealots gut and fuck this pig of a nation as they smile and lie to our faces. I will *not* accept the fact that this happened simply because we've all forgotten that we have more in common than we realize. I will *never* stop trying to get us to look up for a second and realize that those folks you're ranting about on your tiny screens are real people, with real lives, and it may give you a temporary hit of happy when you cut them down, but that depression is going to come screaming back into your face as soon as you take another look at your situation. That's a fact. We need to bury the hatchet, and the best way to do that is to find the motherfuckers more suited for said burial. We need the real enemies—the ones carrying on a tradition of playing us against each other like a chess game in denim and pleather. However, we can't do that until we start talking to each other.

There is nothing on this planet easier than finding all the ways that we are all different. It takes a little more effort to see our shared likenesses anymore, mainly because, like I said before, we don't see things eye to eye. We've reached a breaking point where everything is offensive—*everything*. In the old days, if something was wrong and it offended us, you spoke up, protested, and tried to point out how repulsive it was to the rest of the world, thereby continuing our advancement as humans and as just plain, neighborly folks. Back then there were real issues, like prejudice and racism (which are two different things, people), corruption, and abuse of power. Today we have those same issues, but you can't tell how bad they are because people consider *everything* to be on that offensive level, from the color of your fucking cup at Starbucks to a joke shirt about OCD at Walmart. Let me put it to you this way: you know how you can tell if there's something wrong with your plumbing? The pipes make noises, especially if air gets in the system before you can flush it out. It's like a high-pitched whine of a noise, the Banshee of the Bathroom—squealing like a pig trying out for the opera. It is a shriek from hell, and it is fucking *annoying*. Now, imagine *everything* in your house making that crazy fucking sound, for shitty reasons: someone left the light on in the bedroom (crazy sound), there's a rogue sock left in the dryer (crazy sound), nobody took the garbage out (crazy sound) . . .

See why people just fucking tune out? If social media had perpetual sound, the Banshee Scream is what it would sound like. Although, I believe if social media had actual 24/7 sound, not as many people would have those sites shoved up their asses next to the gerbils and shit-talk. Even if it's something they are strenuously against, they can't take the BS that comes with the whine of the progressives. I know I'll catch some shit for that, but it's true. It's like everyone forgot the story of "The Boy Who Cried Wolf"—IT'S THE SAME DAMN IDEA! I want all of you liberals to pay close attention: putting a cross at the top of a Christmas tree is *not* the same as letting someone get away with using racially or sexually offensive language, like the N-word or the F-word—you know which words I'm talking about. These things should NOT BE PROTESTED WITH THE SAME LEVEL OF OUTRAGE. I get it: the cross does not represent everyone. However, I'm sorry, what other symbol in this day and age would go at the top of the Christmas tree? Hmm? Those are not the same.

This chapter refers to being on the road, and I'll tell you why because it harkens back to the real message I want this book to convey to you. You see, I've been all over the world and back many times over. I've seen beautiful cathedrals in Spain, and I've spun myself dizzy with my kids watching the strobes on the Eiffel Tower in France. I've walked the floors of historic buildings in London and stridden through Red Square in Moscow. I've glutted myself in Tokyo and São Paolo, Sydney and Singapore. I've been all over the world, and yet my favorite country is still my own—largely for the places but also for the people. One of the things these politicians love to beat us over the heads with is how wide the culture gaps are in every state—hell, I as much said so too at the beginning of this chapter, going on and on about our differences. For all intents and purposes, that is indeed true: we range as different as they come, sometimes even within the same state, even the same *city*. But that doesn't mean that (a) we don't have more in common than we'd like to admit, and (b) our differences are something to be looked down upon, ridiculed, or held against us.

That being said . . .

Some of you motherfuckers are absolute morons.

I'm not just referring to one region, state, or demographic. I don't mean only the people who don't know any better. I am not just talking about those of you who support one party or another. I mean—and I don't want you to get this wrong or take it a different way—I mean ALMOST ALL OF YOU. Yes, there is a handful of you out there who are just as fucking flummoxed as I am about the state of this cocked-up union. But I'm not talking to them—I am *screaming* at the rest of you.

I am talking to the fuckholes who bitch, complain, cry, and threaten "celebrities" and "rich folks" for *daring* to care about what happens in their country—then help elect a celebrity "billionaire" cunt who won't show you his taxes, won't talk to the media, *may* have been peed on (hell, who hasn't), and can't tell orange from tan. I'm also talking to the butt-hurt pricks who squeal and accuse people of the most horrendous shit any time they don't get their way. Oh, and lest I forget—I'm *also* talking to the shit heels who have made it *impossible* to have an opinion about *anything* in this country without being labeled a bigot, Nazi, racist, or misogynist dick stain. There is no right side anymore. I used to think there was, and I was wrong. There are officially two sides now: what I believe, and what everyone is shouting directly into each other's faces. That is it. There is *no one party* that represents what I believe anymore, and quite frankly I don't think that party ever existed. It has become the worst case of "I know you are but what am I?" since Sunset Elementary School in Clear Lake, Iowa, 1980. Betsy Smith and Erica Toller went back and forth on the Sunset playground for the better part of an hour and a half, running the gamut from "motherfucking titty asshole shitty" to "lard-licking turd humping garbage face." The epicness of that argument still has not left my memory, and that was thirty-seven years ago. Now imagine that war of/on words raging ON EVERY PHONE IN EVERY HAND IN EVERY HOUSE ON EVERY STREET IN EVERY CITY OF EVERY STATE IN AMERICA . . . AND BEYOND. I had some ass-munch tell me I was a "Killary lapdog." He was from Alberta in Canada—you can't make this shit up, and if you do, there's a good chance you swallowed peyote with dog shit all over it.

But let's be clear right now: if you're a racist cunt, you can go ahead and throw this book in the nearest trash bin at your Klan meeting—you aren't going to like the things I say about you. I'm also going to warn anyone who doesn't like people from other countries: you can give this book to your hippie barista at the nearest Starbucks—I'm going to fucking rip you up too. Oh yeah, I forgot: anyone who thinks you can't be American unless you're white, like white people *only* come from the USA, oh and people who think that Muslims *only* look like Osama bin Laden (maybe not show them the Asian Muslims in the South Pacific . . . or the white Muslims in Croatia . . . or *maybe* just fucking tell them that Muslim is *not a fucking skin color*), yes, if you're one of those people, you should probably avoid this book like a love-in at the NAACP. While we're at it, let's include everyone who thinks that it's mostly black people who are on welfare (not true), it's mostly Latinos and blacks who sell drugs and commit crimes (also not true), and that only nonwhite people commit terrorist acts (Dylann Roof and the Bundy brothers)—yeah, *none* of those fucking people are going to like this book. So if you have a subscription to the Breitbart newsletter, jack off to pics of Milo, or think that a handle bar mustache is just misunderstood, stop reading this book right now. I invite you to either give it away or tear the pages out for TP in your militant prepper bunker because that's the only good you'll get from what's in here.

People pick and choose whether to believe the MSM (mainstream media) based solely on who they're ripping into—*their* candidate or the other guy. Meanwhile real fake news sites incite real violence by making false claims that zealots pick up as fact and spread like herpes on spring break. Not to mention the fact that while *that* is going on, people are choosing whether to discredit our various intelligence agencies, once again, based on whether the info is damaging to Their Guy or The Enemy. Now, I don't expect everyone to be a genius. For fuck's sake, I don't even expect most of you to have a high school diploma because most of the smartest people I know never even finished high school (I didn't either). I'm not asking for this country to be full of Mensa members. But god damnit, I *do* expect people to have some fucking common sense—*especially* the ones who voted for the Cheeto. You were the ones who were certain you had it all figured out, that you were through listening to regular Washington and irregular Hollywood, and you were tired of letting all these so-called bleeding hearts vote against *your* best interest. You are just ordinary family people who don't mind calling a guy "Man of the Year" or telling someone you'll keep them in your prayers, regardless of whether they are actually religious. The salt of the earth are taking back the country. Fine, fine, but you gave it to a bunch of dick bags, man!

They aren't draining the swamp, they'll *never* lock her up, they will never build a wall, and they will never get everyone on the same page about the Affordable Care Act. I'm sorry to say it, but they are going to fuck you over, and I truly, from the bottom of my heart do *not* want them to do that. I don't give a shit about Right or Left, conservative or progressive, traditional or liberal. I care about Americans—all of them. I care about every color, every religion, every ethnicity, and every *life* this country has enabled to be better than it would have been had that life started anywhere else on this giant blue-green billiard ball planet called Earth. I care about rednecks and hippies. I care about yuppies and hipsters. I care about black and white and blue. I care about Asian and Latino and Native. I care about Christian and Muslim and Jewish and Catholic. I care about you *all*—even these gutless bastards in Congress trying to destroy the tiny foothold some people have on life at the moment all because in some way it doesn't jibe with the party line. I care about HRC, and I care about DJT. I care about everybody who can claim this country as his or her own, born or adopted.

Now ask me if I agree with all of them.

Of course I don't. That's my prerogative as an upright animal with sentient thought, and it's also my right as an American citizen. There are two guarantees in our lifetimes: that we will die after we're born and that not everyone is going to think the way we do. Even that statement right there is sure to cause some resentment and angst in many of the shady corners of the chat rooms and message boards out there in the digital revolution above our heads in the analog air: "Well, *actually*, there's no guarantee that you'll be born, so blah blah fuckin' blah . . ." "Only a fascist would say something like *that* blah fuckin' more blah . . ." "TL;DR Corey Taylor should just *stick* to singing . . ." "You call THAT singing? You've obvs never heard . . ." That right there is a conversation between the people who will most likely be running the country someday. If that doesn't make you shit your pants, it's only because you're oblivious to Crazy Town, USA, population HOLY FUCKIN SHITTY BEETS, IT'S EVERYONE. Then you wonder why hard-working people in the Rust Belt and just south of the Mason-Dixon Line look at you like you're all fucking mental patients.

I have a lot to say on the matter, which should come as no surprise to anyone familiar with my work: I *always* have a lot to say about everything. We'll get to all that and more. But I want you to understand this right now: it is *not* my intention to offend any of you. These are merely my thoughts on the United States at present; I am *not* trying to dissuade you from feeling how you feel, and I am not going to try to make a dent in your views either. I am just trying to make some semblance of sense for myself. If I accidentally help one of you put two and two together (it's four, btdubs), it is with your consent and not against your will. I mean, you *did* buy this book, after all. I guess you could've stolen this copy, but there's no need to do that when I'm quite sure a bunch of you will get pissed off and bent out of shape over one fucking sentence in here and it'll end up in the trash or in a half-price bin somewhere. I'm not too worried about it. I half-expect most of my books to be used as kindling anyway. I'm blown away when I find out people actually *do* read these things.

There's a lot of ground to cover here, and I feel like I've procrastinated long enough. Time to get on with it. I've finally found that peace that comes when you eventually see the road in front of you and what you're supposed to do, say, and see. My goal is clear: to bring us all back to the center as I also tell you all why you're wrong, dumb, or both. Only a cunt who cares would be crazy enough to give *that* a shot. Seeing as I'm both of those things, I guess it's as good a miracle as any to try to get by on you. Maybe they'll make me a saint; let's just hope they don't make me a righteous *martyr*. We've come *this* far, Big Money, so we might as well try to hustle our fat asses toward the summit before the sun goes down . . . on *all* of us.

Reminder: above all else, once again, you don't *need* to read this book. You don't need to buy it, borrow it, read it, or believe it. You don't need to give three-fifths of a free shit what I think I know—or claim to, anyway. Chances are you bought it because of the cover or because you know my bands. But once again, I'm not trying to change your minds about how you feel about our country. None of us are ever truly aligned intellectually. We try, but we never get there—that's one of the great things about being human. If you are set in your ways, by all means, continue. If you're unsure about how or what you think or feel, please read on. I just want us all to get down on a couple of things, then I'll be happy, content, pleased as punch.

Overall, this book may not have a happy ending. I know I try to tie my books together with some positivity at the Last Chapter Wrap Parties, but that may not be the case here. This will be a pretty unflinching look at how the United States of America lives and breathes in this day and age. Some of you may not like it. But I hope it'll be something approaching fair. But just like you, I'm going to do my best to be optimistic, not naïve. I'm going to try to be proactive, not so negatively reactive. I'm going to sit all sides down and really try to figure out how the fuck we got here, man. My happy place from the nineties has been harshed so dramatically in the last twenty years that I'm ashamed not of everyone else but of myself. When you take your foot off the gas, the car rumbles to a halt. When you take your eye off the ball, it smashes into your face and breaks your nose. I did both of those things. Hell, I'd say three-fourths of the country did these things. So now it's time to play catch-up and try to make it right or at least get back up to speed so we can try to make things better.

The other option is just sitting back and pretending that it's all an illusion or, worse yet, a dream we're all going to wake up from or, like some of these sleazy cunts, pretend there is *nothing* wrong with this country, that there is no such thing as white privilege, police brutality, or class war, that we can sit back to enjoy more reruns of *Matlock* and *Murder, She Wrote*. I don't know why I picked on those shows—I happen to love *Matlock*, and Angela Lansbury is a goddamn treasure. But anyway, you get the point. You can either engage or enrage, tune in or tune out. Sometimes you get just as much done by doing nothing at all. It'd be like a sit-in if you didn't give a rat's ass about whatever it was you were supposed to be protesting.

That's your right, after all, just as it's my right as an American to bitch about it. Like I said before, it's not going to be pretty, it may not end well, and we may not be friends or even cool with each other by the end of this prickly tome. This is a risk I take any time I commit pure opinion to virtual paper: being quoted and having it come off as holier fact. I don't give a shit if you don't agree with me, to be frank with you. Even if my name is *not* Frank, I still feel this way, and I probably always fucking will. It might turn you into a giant Resting Bitch Face who can't play nice with others. However, if you're up for the journey, sit back, pull on your red-white-and-blue motorcycle helmet, and let's try to find some closure, easy rider.

Don't forget to hold it in once you inhale.

Fuck the fascists.

CHAPTER 2

HOW RONALD REAGAN SAVED CHRISTMAS

WHEN I WAS A KID I TRULY BELIEVED IN SUPERHEROES.

I know. Crazy, right? Sure, I was a kid and all, but I mean it. I believed in superheroes. To me they were as real as everyone else: Spider-Man swinging from building to building, Batman fighting clowns with his mind *and* his fists, Iron Man soaring through the clouds with Superman and Hawkman, the Hulk smashing through the landscape to do battle with aliens—this wasn't fiction. These weren't made up stories. These were news features! In my head the reason they were drawn was because they were so fast that you could never get them to stay still for a real photograph or because with all the explosions and crazy battles going on, no one could *ever* get their cameras to focus correctly. So we had to rely on sketches and illustrations. Hell, they showed drawings of courtrooms and stuff, and *those* people were apparently real, so why couldn't my comic books be as relevant and real as the Sunday *Times*?

Call it youthful naïveté, wishful thinking, parent envy . . . Yours Truly didn't grow up covered in peaches and cream, you know.

But for a while there I believed with all my heart that if I lifted my eyes skyward, I'd see heroes. With or without powers, caped or capeless, smiling, grimacing, winking, frowning, judging—however you wanted to see them, they were out there somewhere, fighting the good fight, protecting the innocent, righting wrongs, settling scores, watching over those who never had anyone to look out for them. They *had* to be real, right? I mean, what good was a world where no one cared whether good could conquer bad? What good was a world where common decency could be killed by extraordinary chaos? The only thing that got me through it all was thinking—*knowing*—that out there in the darkness were great beings with greater power and responsibility, looking for crimes to stop and people to save. Ignorance doesn't always have to be bliss; sadly, it can also be sanity.

As I got older and the abuse kept on coming and yet no one was rushing to my rescue, that idea and those images started to fade until I finally cut them out of my life completely. It's a cold pact to make with yourself, but a necessary one. I learned a long time ago what quite a few survivors learn: hope can make your pain worse, especially when you eventually accept that your knight in shining armor is a two-dimensional character with no possible way of getting to you. Cartoons don't save lives. Men and women in costumes don't really exist, not even now with the so-called real life superheroes who go around in packs of spandex coaxing kittens out of trees and walking grandmothers across streets. That's all well and good, but a YouTube video doesn't actually dispel thirty years of pent-up cynicism and rage. I'm sure some of the inner cities and rougher parts of suburbia could use a few heroes to carry their fucking groceries for them.

Sorry. I know I tend to be one of the more optimistic assholes, but in this case it was a bitter pill to swallow, realizing that none of those fantastic people would save me—or anyone else, for that matter. But I'll tell you an amazing thing that happened: once I wrapped my head around that reality, I decided I was going to protect myself. From that moment on, I was going to defend myself, educate myself, fight and push and work and dedicate myself to never *ever* looking that fear in the eyes again. I swore that I was going to do whatever it took to keep myself safe, and when I had a family of my own I would keep *them* safe. I would make myself stronger and honor my debts. I would learn on my own and live on my own. Sure, it meant becoming a person I wasn't sure I was prepared to be. It meant steeling myself against *too* much sentiment. It meant propping up my backbone with a little bit of false bravado. It meant forgetting most of the lessons that being afraid had taught me. There were times when I didn't think I'd be able to pull it off. Luckily, I had a couple of bands and some talent to help me along the way, working these psychoses on the in- and outside. But I buried a ton of shit as well—shit that I'm only now starting to figure out through therapy. I know: it sounds scary, and it is. But I'm getting through it.

I tell you this story of disillusionment and eventual self-reliance because in so many ways that's exactly how Ronald Reagan became the patron saint of the Republican Party, but in the opposite order of events.

In order to understand how this works, you have to go back and look at where America was in the mid-seventies. Our country had been through some serious fucking shit: several key assassinations, unemployment, gas shortages, undercover CIA work on domestic soil resulting in a massive influx of drugs into the black and Hispanic communities, Watergate, the Cold War—and that's just a short list too; I didn't even get to disco and bell-bottoms. The country had lost its innocence with Vietnam and had been given no time to regain its conscience, instead being destroyed from within by hatred and PTSD. Even when a genuinely good man like Jimmy Carter was elected president, he was saddled with so much debt, inflation, and hopelessness that by the time the USA hockey team beat the Russians at the Winter Olympics, it was a blip on a radar screen that seemed to disappear like a UFO sighting. People wanted something to give them hope again, to feel the happiness they'd felt long ago when things *felt* more optimistic. They wanted a hero.

The Republicans didn't *want* shit—they *needed* a hero. After the fallout from Nixon and the presumption of Ford's idiocy, the GOP was in shambles. Corruption at the highest level had eroded the core idea of conservatism. Their rallying cry of "smaller government" was seen as hypocrisy because of covert break-ins and executive privilege coupled with unconstitutional surveillance. The Right hadn't had a black eye this bad in years. No one wanted to hear them preach about "self-starting." No one could care about states' rights and how they used their funding when everything seemed so bleak. To the country, the Republicans were just as bad as the Democrats: they were all just a bunch of fucking politicians out for themselves.

It didn't help matters that there was no clear idea or vision of what the United States was. The national identity was more regional than anything. Nothing unified us as a country; nothing made us proud to be American. We were at war with what we thought we should be. We weren't like some of our allies: Great Britain had the royals, France was the seat of art and sophistication, Japan had its culture and history. And our enemies were just as well off: the USSR, as it was called (or CCCP in Cyrillic) had Communism, and the Middle East had oil and Allah. America had a tattered flag and a broken promise. Conceptually we were still a baby when it came to being a nation. We had legs—but what the fuck did we *stand* for?

Enter the good governor from California.

Ronald Reagan had been a star in the GOP for quite some time. He originally had been a Democrat but "went Red" in 1962. That makes sense when you remember he was a big film star from Hollywood's Golden Years, and that city is as Blue as they come. Ron and his wife, Nancy, had become the very epitome of class and refinery among the elites in La La Land, and when his film career began to slow down, Reagan found he was a natural for politics. He seemed at ease with the whole "Communist threat" scare tactic that most Republican politicians used in the sixties, balancing such messages by using charm and a mega-watt-power smile to move through the ranks. In the GOP he had the room he needed to be a giant. He easily won the governorship in California and immediately started laying the groundwork for a run at the White House. With the help of some visionaries in the party, he came to represent the look and message of the new Republican Party: the flag, the country western music, the patriotism, the eagles, the working-man persona—our view of the modern-day United States started with the Reagan years.

After two failed attempts at capturing the Oval Office, he finally won by a landslide in 1980. When you look at the circumstances, it makes perfect sense why the other tries shit themselves only to have the third time be the charm—because of a better trailer for a bigger movie. America needed a hero; Reagan was John Wayne with a crisp suit and a fistful of pomade. His nickname was Dutch, and he had a ranch to go with his digs in Washington—I can't tell you how many times I saw the pictures of ol' Ron decked out in his "civvies" while he rode horses out at Camp David. He seemed amiable and jovial, yet there was a toughness in the squaring of his jaw and the squint of his eyes. You could see where years in front of the camera had honed him for the role he was born to play. Hell, he just *looked* like a president. Looking good wasn't a novel idea: people have long thought that Kennedy was the first president to be elected on his fuckability. But with Reagan, there was another aspect that I don't know if anyone else has picked up on: America was not only looking for a hero but also needed a father figure.

The hippies and yippies and mes and yous and whatever else generations were coming into their own, out of the fog of war and the haze of the drug-addled seventies. Suddenly responsibility was being thrust upon men and women no one thought were going to make it out *alive,* let alone make a *living.* They had rejected their own parents out of spite and because of the taut shackles of the fifties. Now they couldn't remember anything past their first joint. Here comes *Bedtime for Bonzo,* a man who looked like he'd help you with your chores and punish you if you got out of line. Reagan could be America's Dad, although at his age, he could've also been our Granddad as well, seeing as he was the oldest president ever elected. So with these ideals thrust upon him, no one stopped to wonder whether his supply-side economic policies would hold water—and, it turned out, they didn't. This so-called Reaganomics model advocated tax reductions for the rich to encourage them to spend more, at which point the profits would "trickle down" onto the lower classes. It didn't work; in fact, the policy has only been shown to really work on a micro level, like a town or small city, not nationally and not even on a state level. Kansas is feeling the unfortunate effects of trying to hold onto that sense of deregulation right now.

Side note: I think the name *Obamacare* is retaliation for naming that economic policy *Reaganomics,* in a way, even though the ACA originated as a *Republican* concept.

The truth is that Uncle Ronnie had some misfires—trickle-down economics, the war on drugs, slashing government spending on everything but the military, fighting public-sector labor, the Iran-Contra affair, bombing Libya, escalating the Cold War by cranking out the missiles in an arms race with the Soviets—even as he had some great moments, like reducing inflation and seeing the gross national product grow annually at a very healthy rate. He also skirted being called two-faced by making his famous speech at the Brandenburg Gate: "Mr. Gorbachev, tear down this wall." The man who'd ramped the fuck out of nuclear weapons manufacturing as a deterrent could now also be credited with helping to bring down the Berlin Wall—not too shabby when you consider that his party had been dead set against the Red Threat for years. Ronald Reagan and David Hasselhoff, fighting the good fight together—now *that* would have been a ticket to believe in.

But I'm an asshole, so what do I know?

The problem started when Reagan couldn't stay president forever—even those of us who didn't like him never really hated him. Sure, my favorite hardcore punk and heavy metal bands at the time all had Reagan T-shirts depicting him in various degrees of degradation. To them Reagan was the enemy, the face of the growing power of the Right, the fascists forcing obedience on a generation that would never be tamed or bought. Being a poor kid, I identified with those bands, not ol' Dutch. So America's dad became the nagging father I'd never had in the first place and now definitely didn't want. Couple that with a Republican governor in Iowa, Terry Branstad, who showed no signs of stepping down (and who, shockingly, has recently been reelected *again*), and I had no love for the GOP.

But once again, never underestimate the power of PR, with lasers and myths and a pyrotechnics display. Reagan may have been going out, but the office was still in their hands; George Bush Sr. was set to rise up from VP to Big P. No more vice president—here comes President Bush (part 1). Bush had the know-how, the experience, and the leadership skills. He even had the Texas knack of getting us into a war right away (a tradition started by Johnson in Vietnam) with the first Gulf War. But he didn't have Reagan's panache. He lacked Ron's ability to, with a wink and a smile, get the American people to roll on down the hill with him on a float made of bald eagles and mountain lions, smothered in flags and fireworks, designed to make sure AMERICA IS MOST, AMERICA IS FIRST! Because of this lack of pop, Bush only lasted one term and ceded to Clinton in the nineties. Then, eight years after that, Bush Jr. picked up the flag and tried stabbing the heart of the dragon, getting into all the shitty things the GOP were now starting to wear on their sleeve.

This was really when the Republican Party's confidence started to shake. It was becoming more and more apparent that the message and the reality weren't the same. Here was a conservative party appealing to the middle and blue-collar class but *actually* using white-collar, multi-million-dollar corporations' influence and money to deregulate everything, driving that same middle class into the poverty zone and putting a bullet in the head of the living wage. But people still stayed with the party for some reason. I believe it has to do with a lot of things: the aforementioned kick-ass special effects of the party that sees no irony in "AMERICA! FUCK YEAH!"; a lack of perceived condescension from, and I quote, "elitists, liberals, and progressive intellectual types"; and zero hesitation to make a show of strength, which would sadly lead to the disgusting bully tactics of the Trump fanatics. We'll talk more about that later, but those are all good reasons to support a party that pretty much shits in the mouth of everything blue-collar America really stands for. Sometimes that "better trailer" is really just the best bits of the movie; the "bigger picture" leaves you pissed off that you wasted your money on such a bag of chopped hog shit.

Fast forward, and now we see ourselves in a world where the GOP is reeling because they allowed themselves to be taken over by a spoiled orange cunt of a human being who *may or may not* have only wanted to run for president so he could promote his new television network, convinced he'd lose the whole time. Well, at least that's what the conspiracy theorists on the Left think. On the Right, they're just shaking their heads. Look a little farther to the right (I won't use that nouveau fucking term those Nazis love), and they're not shaking their heads; they're goose-stepping into a new phase of white supremacy. I have a whole Trump chapter coming up—*that's* how bad he's fucking made it for all of us—but I wanted to paint a clear picture of what happened after Reagan. Thirty-six years later, and we're not just seeing a sullying of "the house that Lincoln built"; we're seeing what happened when we gave in to temptation, when we decided that looks should overrule policy, when we decided that values do not mean nearly as much as winning.

Don't let this chapter fool you: it's not all Reagans and Trumps. There's a certain former president from Arkansas who can be blamed in a lot of ways as well. You see, if Ronnie was the gift of the GOP, then William Jefferson Clinton became the shining star for those Blue devils. I was sure as hell caught up in it. Now at first people just worried that being from Arkansas, Bill Jeff would either (a) come off as a racist dick like that "Dixie-crat" Wallace or (b) get rendered moot by proxy like Carter, even though by then we all knew that Jimmy was something of a goddamn saint. But Bill Clinton—or, as I call him, Clinton I, with Hillary being Clinton

II—fooled us all by appealing to people of every color and having the kind of charm we all wished Carter could've had. Plus, HE COULD PLAY THE SAXOPHONE. We'd never seen anything like it. He could play a fucking saxophone! How the fuck could he do *that?* Presidents aren't supposed to be able to do *anything!*

So I jumped on the Clinton I bandwagon, much like so many conservatives jumped on the Reagan bandwagon, and it was a fun ride! It had rock music and MTV and jobs and the Internet and all kinds of cool things. Clinton was the perfect president for the nineties: young, rebellious, funny, and, dare I say, cool, doing his very best to do the very best for us. We saw an economic boom like we'd never experienced in my lifetime. People were happy—well, Democrats were happy—and it was glaring proof that we didn't need the flag waving and the eagles (even though the Eagles got back together in the nineties too) and all that red-white-and-blue bullshit. We could just be America because it was the greatest country on the planet. We didn't need to rub it in the faces of everyone else—we were too busy living it to lord it over anyone.

Then the fucking bubble burst, literally and figuratively. The dot-com craze made fuckers rich *and* poor all within the same minute. Republicans didn't like Clinton I's diplomacy and the way he handled certain foreign crises, specifically Somalia, and once they regained control of Congress in 1994, the standoffs began, shutting the federal government down *twice*. Then a cigar, a confession, and a dirty, *dirty* dress led to the Lewinsky chronicles. Although he wasn't impeached, it fairly killed Clinton's credibility. When he left office all he'd done was make it harder for Dems to get elected for a while. This is the most disappointing bit because he was, in my opinion, just as good a president as Reagan was. Clinton I had an economic surplus at one point—something that hadn't happened in the United States since the sixties. Clinton I, much like Reagan, was a fitting symbol of the times: good natured, meaning well, but ultimately flawed and only human after all. This realization has brought me to a conclusion and a question. My conclusion is that we don't vote for the party but the person. You can argue that all you want, but it's true. The one who wins is almost always the one people like the most. And if this *is* true, then here's my question: If we're just voting for the one we like the most, then why the fuck do they even need political parties at all?

I know it makes things easier. I know most of us can't even be bothered to memorize an ATM pin number half the time, let alone give a shit about certain policies and whatnot, so it does make it easy: Republicans are *supposed* to be for smaller government, lower taxes, more rights for the states, and conservative values like "pro-life" and "good Christian morals" and "family values." Democrats are the futurists, the ones who believe in freedom, in taking care of each other and themselves, with big government helping us along the way, creating laws that maintain freedom, not block it, and guarantee equality for all, no matter what—pro-choice, pro-love, all colors, all people. These two parties, which have been our parties since the mid-1800s, with very little outside threat of being replaced (sorry, Bull Moose and Tea Party), have been Our Government for so long that we just take it for granted. Actually, let me rephrase that: *they* take *us* for granted. They just know that because they have most of the money and the commercials, we'll be forced to vote for who *they* want us to vote for. But at this point in the game I haven't seen anything to show me that these parties are coming up with anything new. So what does it matter which party they come from? Why not put a little more emphasis into likeability and charm?

I'll tell you exactly why, and what went down in the Democratic primaries fairly played that out: because as long as they have the money, politics is a *business*. The Democratic National Committee got caught fucking over Bernie Sanders in favor of Hillary Clinton. This is highly unethical, and it was made even more embarrassing by the fact that Bernie was *the shit*. Bernie was *my* pick. I didn't care if he was old as Christ, I didn't care that he turned purple when he was riled up, and I didn't care that he was an Independent who'd only joined the Democrats so he could run for president. Bernie Sanders is a no-BS, top-notch guy who has been fighting against financial waste and civil rights corruption for years. He was my dude—shit, he was everybody's dude. The people at the DNC knew it too, so they pulled some crazy shenanigans to fuck him over. It's still not clear how much Clinton II knew about it, but the fact of the matter is that *the party* was responsible for that, just as the Republican Party was responsible for allowing Trump to go as far as he did on the platform and violent message he was spewing. Those parties, in my opinion, have put themselves in front of who the candidate turns out to be, which, I'm sorry, is just silly. I don't vote Republican or Democrat; I vote based on who I am, which just happens to be a little bit of both. I am convinced that is the way most Americans are: fuck the fringes, the leaf-eaters, and the bigots—fuck them. I'm talking about everyone else in our country, the people who are in no hurry to join a group. That's America, the ones behind closed doors making decisions based on real life. So if most Americans aren't *really* as clear as they have registered, then why have these antiquated political parties, run by fanatical fuck heads on million-dollar payrolls? If we know we're going to vote for the person we *like*, let's start from scratch. Let's ditch these two old-ass parties and figure out what the future should look like.

That's essentially what happened with Reagan and Clinton I. Reagan represented the New Conservative: family values and freedom; good, clean, and wholesome all wrapped in a flag like a pig in a blanket, with some fiscal mismanagement thrown in for good measure. Clinton I was the same, adhering to a new Democratic Party line called the *Third Way,* which tried to come more toward the center and, in turn, become more conservative while also maintaining its stance on human rights. Politicians have moved and modified old stances for years, so it's not without precedent. But I feel like we don't need any of that shit. What we need is a whole new set of plans and rules. You want this government to go back to when it was more "of the people, for the people, by the people"? Then have I got a plan for you, my friends. Listen up, because I'm only going to run this down for you once. It may *sound* crazy, but there's a thin line between crazy and creative, even if the minds behind these types of ideas tend to hang themselves from these thin lines. But I have an idea and a solution.

There are four years between presidential elections. That means there are four years we could spend looking for a better option as our leader. So I believe a great idea would be to use these four years to scour the entire country—every coast, every state, every city, and every suburb—until we find people to run against each other. We put together gangs of hopefuls and use the Internet and TV to choose the ones we really like. Then we whittle *those* down until we get the number to ten people. Then those ten people take it upon themselves to "campaign" for a year, leading up to a "Great Choosing" in which, much like all those shitty singer reality TV shows that ruin television and music simultaneously for me, we *let America nominate* based on text voting, which, at this point, I'd have to think is just as reliable as actual booth voting. America nominates the two they like the most, then the race is on. For sixty days the two "people's nominees" debate and talk and answer questions *together,* all around the country. Then we vote for who gets to be president for four years. But here's the kicker: there aren't really any losers because the one who isn't voted president becomes vice president, the other eight left over from the original ten are part of the cabinet, and anyone else from the original round-up becomes a special ambassador for their states in *both* houses of Congress—Senate *and* the House of Representatives—to remind those career politicians about the will of the people who put them there in the first place. A truly democratic government should never forget that the populace it governs could replace it in an instant.

I can already see the social media sites condemning me to a seething, fiery death with snakes and ladders and shit. "Scoff scoff," they'll say, "The Dishonorable Mr. Taylor has no idea how the truly democratic process works! A system of such putrescence would *never* work in this day and age, sinking underneath the sheer weight of its own ridiculousness." To which, obviously, I would reply with: Why? Why is their method of choosing a presidential candidate any better than what I just put out there as an idea? We've already established that people within the DNC got up to no good when it came to picking theirs, and I'm going to go on record with absolute certainty that the RNC regretted the day they took that ass-cannon Trump seriously. These were both under the current system of putting forth the "best of our two-party system." Like them or not, they were regarded as the two worst choices for the presidency in God Knows How Long (an actual measurement of time, used by the Mayans on their circular calendar, referring to "the last time White Man seemed to have their collective shit together").

So there's my idea for what to do about this whole president fiasco. I know what most of you are going to say: "Hey shit fucker, stick to singing, and leave the politics to professionals," or, "Nothing pisses me off more than when an entertainer who has no business talking about politics talks about politics." To which I usually reply, "You just described the dude you most certainly voted for, you rustic pussy whistle." But you know me: I dislike irritation on a cerebral level. I also hate people who make me feel that just because I have had some success in my life and been able to make some money, that suddenly I am NO LONGER QUALIFIED OR WELCOME to talk about politics in my country. That is such a fucking bullshit cop-out of a response to something you don't agree with, and it really fucking bothers me that so many people get away with it. These are usually the same people who bragged about "lurking around polling stations to intimidate people who aren't voting Trump." Can you believe that, in 2016, certain Americans find they need to resort to tactics perfected by the brown-shirted Nazis in the 1920s? My only comfort is that people aren't standing for it. Americans have had enough of the bullying and are pushing back.

Reagan wouldn't have felt good about that either. Of all the Republican presidents in my lifetime, I think he understood people the most. He understood that you don't keep a country running by dividing it; you keep it running by bringing people together and keeping them there. That's why most successful politicians don't claim the Right *or* the Left but work the center. That's where the world is, in a nutshell. Yes, it's true that we have some fringe fuckers who are as certifiably fucked up as a football bat, but the majority of us are very much huddled together in the middle of it all, the center where the good ideas on both sides collide and commingle. Successful politicians know that when it comes to crowds of people, you run the "hits"—rhetorical ideals, essential appeal, and the overall message. But when you break it down on an individual level—the person just sitting there in his or her own head (and Spider-Man PJs)— you hit them with the center because that's where we *all* live if you're worth a shit as a human being. We all have more in common than we are different, no matter what they say to "break up the band." Yes, we're prone to extremes, but not all extremes are hate and racial and fiscal and conservative and progressive and peaceful and warmongering and whatever; sometimes those extremes are just a severe hankering for double chocolate fudge ice cream.

Reagan was one of the best at understanding this about America. He could fire the horns of FUCK YEAH, REPUBLICAN GUNS, GOD, AND FLAG SHIT, getting the crowd whipped into a frenzy and ready to vote Red. Then he could turn around and talk with Democrats, find a common interest, empathize from their standpoint, and incorporate that into the policy, shaping something originally conservative, implying the liberal bits, and coming to a bill that was suddenly central in nature. This is why he was able to work with Tip O'Neill, the Democratic Senate majority leader. The name of the game, ol' Dutch knew, was *compromise*. Compromise has been the cornerstone of American politics since the beginning. Now some of you may be saying "horse pucky," but it's true. It's a slower process, but it ensures that the will of the people is being done. It's a slow process precisely because of the will of the people—there's no one right way to correctly sum up the will of the people. Might as well call it the will of the zeitgeist.

We are a nation of ids and idiots sometimes, and it takes a while to sift through the damage to find the diamonds.

It's now 2017, and the spirit of Ronald Reagan permeates everything that armchair Republicans wish for their party: a knowing smile, a strong hairline, a square jaw to go with what they consider a square deal—conservatives always had better imagery to work with. With liberals it's hard to get ideals and ideas to stick to a rockin' poster. Conservatives got the whole enchilada and the hot sauce to smother it. So I can see why they cling to Reagan—he looked like their leader. Sadly, that's not the case these days. More and more the Right are being left with what can only be described as a bunch of fucking temp workers who couldn't cut it in the Klan: none of the charm, *none* of the background or common ground, but *all* the stubborn stupidity that comes with thinking you're right and refusing to listen to facts, figures, or fate. I'm not just saying this because I disagree with a lot of what they say—they are just SO FUCKING CONCEITED that they think they can just bluster and bloviate and eventually people will get worn out and give in. But it doesn't work that way anymore. People are sick of fear tactics. People are sick of being intimidated. They're sick of being beat over the head with a fistful of poison politics that only helps the top 1 percent under the guise of speaking for the working man.

Lord knows they've searched for the Second Coming of Bonzo. Romney didn't work, though he came close to looking the part (I always got more of a Bond villain vibe from him, to be honest), McCain and Dole were just a bit too old, and Dubya had the charm (which is why he was elected twice, I suppose) but none of the respect or old-school strength. But with each passing decade they get more and more desperate. Case in point: Mike

Pence, the caustic ex-governor of Indiana, now vice president, in favor of fiscal fallout and conversion therapy—you know, the Christian method of "helping" young adults who are homosexual by torturing them until they give up on their identity just so the pain will stop. Sounds wonderful, doesn't it? That shows you how far down the fucking rabbit hole you have to be if *that cat* is a viable candidate for vice president on your ticket. Now you're not even in the same hemisphere as the party of the 1980s. Now you've suddenly entered the world of legislating to taste—kind of like putting a giant statue of the Bible in front of the courthouse and assuming there will be no bias against you if you don't subscribe to their version of God.

I'm trying not to get angry here. This book is supposed to be balanced in message and humor. So far I haven't said a lot that you could laugh at, but that's because I haven't really written about anything funny yet. I keep pushing off the funny shit because I always figure there's time for jokes as long as you make your point first. Maybe I feel like I haven't made my point yet. Where the fuck was I going with this, anyway? I started with superheroes, moved on to Ronald Reagan, encapsulated the drowning image of the political idol shape, and segued nicely into the relative death of socioeconomic worship. Johnny Thunders sang, "You can't wrap your arms around a memory," and I think that's where I was going. I think that's where the Republicans have it fucked. They've been wrestling a ghost with the strength of a giant boa constrictor for nearly forty years. Reagan was amazing for them because he worked in that moment in time. He was a reflection of what America needed to feel like and what we needed to see ourselves as in the long run. After that, there has been very little in the way of evolution or diversity for their party. Yeah, every once in a while they'll trot out their token minority for their fucking

State of the Union rebuttal or to attack POC with a different line of bullshit. But the Republican Party has only stagnated because they only represent a very specific part of the country. Albeit, they've won the White House (barely), but that's not how our politics grow. That's why the Democrats were the first to elect a black president—because these are more accurate views of what America is and wants to be. How is it that the party that freed the slaves became the party that now treats people like slaves?

Maybe it's the optimist in me, but I feel like the collapse of the GOP can be a good thing. I know on the surface it seems like a catastrophe for people who think they're true-Red 'Pubs, branded in America for the good of freedom and pancakes and shit. That's not being a Republican; that's just being American, a very specific version of American. The Right used that shit to get you, even though they haven't identified with that in years, if they ever did at all. Like I said before: if you checked the laundry of the GOP, every collar would be more white than blue and dirtier than any other party on the planet. So it's good that their lies have folded in on themselves. From those ashes can come something a little more honest, ambitious, kosher, a little closer to the center we've always wanted. Maybe back to basics: freedom for everyone regardless of color, religion, sex, or history. Or maybe just back a few decades: self-starters welcome, help for the independent businesses, and money in your local communities. Maybe this time they'll keep religion out of the laws they try to pass. Maybe they'll keep their unbelievably antiquated views on race out of their legislation—or better yet, maybe they'll *listen!* Listen to *why* this prejudice is unwarranted and *unwanted.* Listen to why the world cannot afford to think and live this way anymore. There are beautiful people and shitty people in every color under the sun. Singling out one shade is just pathetic.

You can't be this blind to what you've become, conservatives. You are officially every cliché in *Footloose*. You can't have missed that. It's why you only appeal to one color—LILY FUCKING WHITE—and very little to basically EVERY OTHER ONE OUT THERE. You didn't used to care—historically speaking, white people were really the only ones who came out to exercise their right to vote. When it seemed like other colors were starting to ramp up a resistance by voting another way, you did everything from changing voting laws to realigning voting districts to maintain power. But you can't do that anymore. People are on to you. Now your laws are being overturned because—BIG FUCKING SHOCK—they are unconstitutional. Now voters are coming out in droves, mainly because you allowed a fucking imbecile to be your nominee but also because you've spent a lot of years having it your way and ensuring that everyone else gets screwed. So the people are speaking. Actually, they're screaming—at *you*. So now that your party is in tatters, it's time to shape up. If you want any future of trying to do good for the American people, you need to remember that there are A LOT OF DIFFERENT AMERICAN PEOPLE. If you can't get that through your fucking head, THEN OFF WITH YOUR FUCKING HEAD.

I'll keep some faith, though. I grew up in the Midwest, so there's a part of me with a certain conservative bent, just as I realize that a few forms of welfare can and have helped people who could use the lift up off the ground. After all, I was one of those people. I was a child of food stamps and Reagan cheese giveaways. I am a product of school lunches and holiday sponsors (programs in which rich people take kids out and buy them presents). I've seen the other side—I know that it's not all succubi and leeches. Those in charge love sweeping terms because it sucks the humanity completely out of the "who and why" these programs help. I'm not one of those people who believes healthcare can just be free, not in a free market and a capitalist nation. But I do think that there is no real reason why platforms can't exist to get some folks back on their feet again. Sure, these programs need policing so the thieves who try to work the system are dealt with. But we are so capable of empathy and kindness, especially to our own people dealing with adversity. We forget sometimes that this is about helping Americans. I think Reagan would agree with me that taking care of our own is a far better legacy to leave behind than pulling us all apart from within and from without. The pain judges us all; there are no exceptions on this point. We can either reach out a hand or turn our backs. I fail to see any other option.

Uncle Ronnie wouldn't want that. I'm not sure how he'd feel about Trump at the helm, but he wouldn't want us giving the cold shoulder to the American people. At the end of the day that man bled red, white, and blue. He wasn't the hero we wanted at times; however, he is an iconic figure for a reason: because he dared to pull us up off the floor and got us to stop feeling sorry for ourselves. That was no easy feat. I *think* that's what so many of us would like for ourselves now. Reagan is gone, Trump can't do it, and there's really no one left. I guess I'll keep scanning the horizon for a better choice. I hope you'll join me.

CHAPTER 3

RED, WHITE, AND BLUETOOTH

TODAY I'M WRITING TO YOU FROM THE DISTANT PAST.

Well, not *so* fucking distant, really—at the most we're probably only talking about a year or so ago. Still, that's a fucking weird one, isn't it? Almost like a sort of reverse time travel. "OOOOOOH, TAKE HEED, O LEERY WAYWARD TRAVELER! FOR IIIIIIIII HAVE BEEN TO THE PAST, AND I AM ABOUT TO REGALE YOU WITH INCREDIBLE THINGS YOU MOST LIKELY WOULD HAVE PUT TOGETHER ON YOUR OWN ANYWAY. YEAH, NOT REALLY A REVELATION, BUT STILL! OOOOOOOH!" I can just see people lining up for my futuristic ride at Disney's California Adventure now. Everybody hold on to your dicks and experience "Corey Taylor's Trip into Just a Little Bit Ago!" Fuckin' *magic*. If I were a big enough cunt to write with emojis, this is where the Magic Floating Head would roll his eyes. Plus, when you think about it, *all* books are written from the past, which kind of pops the cherry on my so-called brilliance when it came to this vision. That bums me out—I truly thought I was being clever. Tells you what's wrong with *me*, I guess . . .

It's a CMFT book—there's was *bound* to be a paragraph that went screaming off the tracks . . .

Anyway, getting back to my DIY blast from the past, I want to describe to you the epiphany I had not too long ago. You see, I was visiting a far-off land of exotics and mystery on the last Slipknot tour. It was a place I thought I'd never get to go to because some of the politics surrounding this place don't quite jibe with America's way of life—not the country itself but one of its "benefactors." So for a long time it seemed like this wouldn't be a possibility. Then suddenly one thing leads to another, an offer we couldn't refuse came across our desks, and bada boom bada bing, we were working its capital city into our routing. I for one was excited! I love going places I've never been before. When we arrived it was nighttime, so we didn't get to go out and explore very much, but I was confident we'd be out and about once we all got some much-needed shuteye.

Cut to my reaction when I got to my hotel room. The only way I can make you understand what I was feeling was that the entire place smelled like the seventies. There was a war for supremacy being waged between the stink of a few decades' worth of cigarette smoke and the specter of an overflowed bathtub sunk deep in the rug. It was a heavy stink—the kind of stink that stays with you through at least two washes, understand? It was the kind of stink that might turn you on if you were into certain kinds of kink. The bed was no better—for some reason my pillows reeked of a backed-up toilet with every other breath. Yeah, you read that right. Every *other* sniff was terrible. I don't know where the hell that nasty shit would go when I was prepared for it, but motherfucker, it would come rushing back into my defenseless nostrils when I wasn't . . . um, nose looking. There's an odd situation: How *would* you describe a smell you didn't "see" coming? And what sort of phrase would fit that scenario? There's nose-blind or nose-deaf, but is there such a thing as nose-ignorant? Ooh! What about *in-sniff-erent?* That's a great one! I was becoming in-sniff-erent to the barrage of stankins going on around me. I drew a reluctant breath and resolved to ride out the night, and I'd figure it out in the morning.

The next morning a storm hit the island—because of *course* it did. I was locked in all day: no trips to any of the islands, no walking around the thoroughfares or marketplaces, no seeing any of the sites of historical significance—just a gray backdrop to the assault on my nose's Thirteenth Precinct. There are a lot of words I can come up for this scenario: insufferable, intolerable, grossly unfortunate. However, all that kept coming to *my* mind was, "Well, *fuck,* man!" Suffice it to say it was a long fucking four days stuck in that particular predicament. Now, you may be screaming at yourself to ask me, "Hey toots, what's the matter with a little rain? Afraid to get wet, are ya?" To which my most furtive reply would be, "Stick your shitty questions back up your ass, cocksucker—in blue *and* black ink, thank you very much." Honestly, you only have yourself to blame for that one—you *know* I'm a fucking asshole.

Anyway, as I sat there in that far-off land, nestled among the stiff sheets, the dank, retched smells, and the isolation brought on by the color gray reflecting and bouncing around every corner of the room, I closed my eyes and thought to myself, *Even with all the issues going on, I cannot WAIT to get back to my country.* And *that,* my friends, is how awesome the United States can be: when even the lure of a rain-drenched exotic island can't compare to being able to do whatever the fuck you want at any time of day. I'm not going to sit here and pretend that this feeling has been extended to everyone in our country; unfortunately, certain fuckwads are trying to ruin it for a lot of people because to *them,* WHITE ONLY = AMERICAN. We'll talk about that in a little bit, but for the time being let's discuss America like it's fair and balanced for us *all.* This country can be fucking Candy Land with the right method and mayhem, especially when you take into account that there are *no* closed borders between states (except the one out in the middle of Canada), *no* curfews in the major cities (except where the populace exercises their rights to peaceably protest), *no* limit to what you can do with your money (except buy and distribute drugs, and then only in states where it's not legal yet). I mean, you can eat, fuck, work, smoke, dance, run, laugh, live and die twenty-four hours a day in the Greatest Country in the World™.

Yeah, I put the trademark symbol on that fucker. We rub that in people's faces so often that we *have* to own the rights to that saying. Plus, I'll be honest: it's hard to argue with the reasoning behind our odd proclamation. You need to remember this is the same United States where the United Nations sent an envoy to review how the indigenous people protesting the Dakota Access Pipeline were being treated while in custody. Yes, you read that right: while protesting, the Native Americans and their allies were being abused in ways that were so bad that the UN—an organization that goes to places like Syria and Iran to investigate abuses or acts of war—CAME TO AMERICA. That's how *bad* it's gotten for certain people. Between Black Lives Matter and #IStandWithStandingRock, this country looks a lot more like Nazi fucking Germany sometimes than it does the freest country on Earth. Like I said, if your skin color is a little bit darker than see-through pale, chances are you're going to get fucked over in the USA. We the people who give a shit are trying to beat it back, but it's gotten out of hand. I think we all know why, but once again, we'll cover that in an up-and-coming chapter.

Disturbing flaws and hypocritical laws aside, if you play your cards right in America, you can go a long way. Some places are more liberal than others, and it's easier for everyone to find a way to get ahead. Speaking from experience, if you're going to be homeless somewhere, make it America in the summertime, or at *least* in the Southwest or on the West Coast. That's not a joke; that's a fucking *fact,* tested and ratified by This Guy Doing the Writing. There are institutions set up and designed to get you fed, get you some clothes, get you a place to sleep, and so forth. Right down the line, they'll take care of you—not because they *have* to but because they really actually fucking give a shit whether you live or die. Some of these armchair conservatives want to talk shit on the "bleeding hearts," but those bleeding hearts kept me alive, so go fuck yourselves, thank you very much. Just goes to show you: even if you ain't got a motherfucking thing in America, you can STILL GET SOME SHIT in America.

I've seen a motherfucker with no house walking around with a cell phone. That's how easy it is to stay on top of shit in this country. Either he's brilliant or I'm an idiot. Then again, both of those statements can be true. I know the pendulum swings both ways and cuts everybody. For every person stuck in a system trying to get help, there's a genius bastard using the system to help his or herself, screwing everyone else over in the process. Best-case scenarios have these grifting bastards being caught before they can siphon too much away. The worst-case scenarios involve scandal, prosecution, and eventually shutting down these programs because "it just goes to show you that the welfare state is a lie—just a bunch of people who don't want to work for a living."

You could say that's the problem with the system, but it's also an example of the ingenuity that comes with a free country. If these fuckers had put as much work and thought into working and doing something with their lives as they had in manipulating a system designed to help people who can't help themselves, maybe we'd be a little better off in the end. Of course, there are people who believe a fiscally balanced country wouldn't have room for certain welfare programs like these, to which I'd say, "Yeah, and just how much does your budget give to the military and religious legislation again?"

This, however, is the price we pay for entitlement and technology: laziness to progress and impartiality to the plight of others. Yes, this kind of free thought in a free market can lead to incredible discovery and investment. It can also lead to shit heels "doing a run" on food stamps. I'll explain: food stamps can only be used for food—or at least that's the way it *used* to be. So people on food stamps who want to use the money for other things—like cigarettes, gas, bills, and so on—"do a run" on the books as they come in by splitting them up between friends or family members, sending them into various stores, using them to buy something for $0.10 to $0.25, collecting the change—in real currency—and consolidating it into cash to be deposited in a checking account or blown on booze and drugs. I've seen it both ways—this is just a *minor* scam. I've also seen some shit that is so fucking disturbing that it'd put you off trying to help people for thirty fucking years. So I'll just save those for my memoirs.

If you think these *are* my memoirs, shit, just wait until the ones who can testify are dead . . .

There are ways to circumvent the various welfare states in the United States, but there are also several ways to get up on your feet from a small business standpoint. There are federal grants for these things and tax breaks for starting local businesses. Hell, this is the *only* fucking country I can think of where little corner markets can change hands quite a few times, from people who've lived here their whole lives to people who just showed up, and boom, you've got a way to feed and take care of your family. Bodegas and corner shops have been a nice steady source of revenue for ages. I know of families who've just wandered into *abandoned* shops, gotten the power turned back on, lined up distribution, and before anyone can cry, "How the fuck did you get the keys for this place?" they're well and embedded, with no way to supplant them according to squat laws. Isn't that crazy? I know little white fuck-offs who bitch and moan because they have to actually pick up shit at the makeup counters they work for (part time), and yet here are these resourceful families coming into a place they've never been and being afforded a way of life based on some shit they've never felt before: freedom.

That's why some of us pasty heathens are such dick lickers—we take our freedom for granted and feel threatened when (a) people remind us of how amazingly we have it so we pump up some piddly shit to feel "burdened" and (b) we find out somebody might actually be better off than we are, and because we can't have that, seeing as we're "white and right," we cry foul for some trumped-up shit (see what I did there?). Don't believe me? Ask some white motherfucker with a big mouth and an incredible sense of entitlement what's so offensive about the BLM movement. They'll either claim it's a terrorist organization trying to kill us all or they'll get defensive and start throwing around that "All Lives Matter" horseshit, which is just them admitting that, yes, people have it way worse than we do in this country, but because we can't handle that sort of guilt, we'll be sanctimonious and make ourselves look like cunts by demeaning and downplaying the importance of the real problem. These are the days in which we live, folks: when white people *still* can't *stand* the fact that people of color still have it way fucking worse than we do, so we cry "reverse discrimination" to keep from crying in our gold-plated mashed potatoes. It's times like these when the whole gaggle of fuck-holes should seriously consider just shutting the fuck up.

That's because white people have never required a reason for anything—just justification. White people—not all, but several—are *very* good at playing both sides of the fence for their own purposes: slave/master, oppressor/oppressed, and victim/anything that has to do with assault of *any* kind. We've been doing this sort of thing since we decided that white people should be in control. We are the kings of privilege; our slighted hands are simply sleight of hand. We can exaggerate our problems for the sake of the argument just so we're not seen as being too opulent, which, to be fair, isn't something anyone should be made to feel bad about. But that shit comes and goes as well. The same people who bitch and moan about a celebrity's opinion on politics are the same people who'll act high and mighty when it comes to any sort of programs that get people back on their feet. Then again, maybe they don't like the fact that most people on welfare are white. So much for "we work harder than those other colors." Maybe that's why they also like to try to restructure districts and regulations to make it harder for people of color to vote properly. White politicians don't like activism because it's a reminder of how shitty our track record has been with progressive change. It's a child's argument: "Well, *she* started it!" Social media has cranked the volume knob on this particular Marshall head, but it's been around for ages.

Sorry if I offend any white people with these sentiments, but being as I'm also white and I've seen this type of reprehensible shit firsthand, you should probably put that faux offense away for a bit. I'm going to make a point, albeit eventually. So let me circle back to something I said before in an earlier chapter. One of the things white people love to do is claim that black people can be racist as well. That's not accurate, and if more people knew what the actual definition of racism was, maybe we could get a better handle on it. No, white people have it all wrong. Some black people aren't racist—they are prejudiced. Prejudice is about a certain hatred that comes with a preconceived notion about the color of someone's skin or gender or sexual preference. It stems from sweeping, shitty stereotypes, like "all black people are criminals," or "all Latinos are in gangs," or "all gays are child molesters," or "all white people are Nazi skinheads." Do you see what I mean? That is prejudice: a conclusion made based on garbage. Racism is very different. Racism has to do with control and a very certain kind of imagined control. Racism is the belief that one race is far superior to all other colors, shapes, and sizes and that not only do people of this race have the right to do whatever they want to people but that those other colors are expected to bow down and succumb, kneel, yield, concede, and all that bullshit. *That* is racism. Black people don't do that. They stick up for their culture and almost certainly amplify their pride based on hundreds of years of oppression and opposition, but even if they feel and believe that being black is better than being any other color, that's not the same thing as racism. White people have a very different approach to those sentiments. They will steamroll you with their believed superiority even when they don't think they're racist themselves. It's kind of amazing to watch sometimes, this battle between "peace over privilege." But that's my point: white people even have to make a conscious effort to fight a weird inherent mindset that somehow we *are* better than everyone else. It could just be that we humans are all psychotically egotistical and that everyone else is just better at keeping it in check than white folks. Time will tell.

I know what you're thinking right now: *Is this book just going to be a roast of white people? Where's all the funny shit? Uncle Fuckmouth, where's all the funny shit?* Well, brothers and sisters, there will be some funny shit somewhere in here, but first we've got to set the record straight. We've got to make sure there is a baseline pulse on this hot-ass topic. It's essential not only to the struggle but also to our sanity. In the *real* world there is no such thing as "alternative facts"; there are just LIES LIES LIES, YEAH. If you're asking, that is, of course, my favorite song from the Thompson Twins—great track. Sorry—I got away from the subject there for a second, started singing that song, and suddenly I was running downstairs for the dryer and the Aqua Net, ready to spruce, spritz, and spray. It has been a long time since I rocked my guy-liner for some musical hijinks. Christ, we're still talking about this, aren't we? I tend to forget my starter topic right around the time the paragraph begins to look like the continent of Australia . . . or is that the country of Australia—fuck it: it's both. Is this thing on? Testicles: one . . . two . . . three!?

One of the perks of white privilege has always been the rewriting of history, which is exactly why Trump has been so desperate to rewrite even his most *recent* history, his search history, *anything* to make it look like he's more popular than he really is. He's not the first to do it, though. However, it must be a white American thing because we even got who discovered America wrong. Columbus never set foot on our end of North America; the closest he got was Hispaniola. It's the same story with the settlers in Plymouth. The history books love to paint the first natives of this land as dumb and unsophisticated, but the truth of the matter is that Squanto, the first native to meet the settlers, spoke English. You read that right: he spoke English. It turned out he'd been kidnapped by buccaneers years before and taken back to Europe. He managed to gain his freedom and make his way to England, where he spent some time before he was able to jump a ship and head back to the "New World." In that time he'd learned several languages. So it was almost perfect for the pilgrims that he happened to be there. But of course, like it or not, we got all "white" on them and condemned their ways of life to a long, drawn-out death. Thankfully that hasn't happened yet, but you get my meaning: for some reason we honkies have a hard-on for trying to correct motherfuckers just minding their own fucking business. What did the original missionaries really do? Try to get indigenous peoples to abandon their own "false gods and prayers" in favor of the *whiter* "false gods and prayers." You see it all the time, sadly.

The backlash of this whitewashing is very apparent, though, even today. Twenty-four hours hadn't even passed after the post-Inauguration Women's March before people were complaining about the police's stance toward what was considered a "white women's privilege march," and we're talking about a historic movement that spanned the globe on *all* seven continents, including Antarctica. Even in the face of amazing solidarity for *all* colors, people had to find a way to talk shit. I'm not saying I don't understand—hell, I'm not even saying they aren't right. But Judas fucking Priest, save that shit for later. It's fucking bad enough that the current administration has to send their babbling press people out to defend shitty turnout for their "historic victory." Do you really think it's necessary to divide us even further? But once again, this is the by-product of the collision between freedom of speech and social media. Just because you have the right to say it doesn't mean we have to listen, even if you type that shit in all caps. Sorry, Beavis.

We also love to fuck with the books when it comes to making ourselves look better. If you were to ask certain Trump supporters why they voted for him in the first place, a lot of them would say it's because he's going to help with job growth (even though under the Obama administration job growth was exponentially steady for his eight years in office). When prodded about social programs like welfare, they will blind you with a lot of rhetoric about people of any color under the sun being on food stamps and whatnot . . . except white people. "All the blacks, Mexicans, even Asians—they're *all* on welfare! They're suckin' our government *dry.*" They love to trot that little misconception out there. I say *misconception* because a study published by the *Huffington Post* in 2013 showed that white people—*white people*—receive more food stamps and welfare benefits than African Americans, Latinos, Asians, and the entire "other" column—*combined.* Maybe that's our blessing and curse as Caucasians: we're only noble when we're missing the facts. Hell, even my computer is kind of racist. It automatically capitalized the word *Caucasian.* However, when I typed in "Latino" or "Asian" without capitalizing, the Red Line of Correction showed up, suggesting I capitalize those words, but not doing it for me. Is that a good enough metaphor for you?

Listen, I don't want you to think I hate my people. I don't. I also know there's a huge double standard in this country in which certain people cannot talk about certain things without being called every name in the liberal book. It's called "real talk" for a reason, but if it's real talk, why aren't we all allowed to be real with it? As I've said before, there are words I will never use because I do not like the tone, the history, the hate connected to them and the feel of them crossing my lips. That being said, if it's in a conversation about race or out of context, without an accusatory tone, why aren't those words allowed to be used while talking about progression? The last time I checked, the only way to take the venom out of our vocabulary was to beat the shit out of the context until those words are nothing more than snake skins lying on flat hot stones. Making them taboo does nothing more than add a sense of adventure and excitement to their use, building the first bridge between risqué speech behind closed doors and violent defamation in a public display of violence. You may think I'm a doomsayer by making that jump, but then again, maybe you've forgotten what it's like to be a kid sneaking a smoke behind the school or drinking your first beer. I'm not comparing racist remarks to rebelling against authority; I'm comparing it to the shit we were all told was off-limits when we were kids. I believe that's one of the reasons we find ourselves in the situation permeating the world today: when you make certain speech forbidden, you simultaneously make it attractive. It's human nature. Don't believe me? Then answer this: Who was the last person to smoke a cigarette based on tobacco's health benefits?

I rest my fuckin' case.

But that's the USA M.O. really, isn't it? Hypocrisy has always been more American than freedom. We talk a good game but never really back it up. The double-talk knows no lines, no sides, and no bipartisan loyalty. We are a country full of monstrous two-faced dicks, hell-bent on fucking each other over because all we want to be is *right*. That's all we want. Hell, I'd dare say that's exactly how the Cheeto got elected in the first place. In addition to hoping he would get a handle on the fiscal spending of the government, most of the working class were just tired of being told they were *wrong*. That mentality runs all the way up the flag pole, right next to the stars and stripes themselves, and it only intensifies the further one gets from the eye of the storm. The Right wants to tell you what you can and can't do with your body, especially your Mommy Parts, but can't seem to keep it in their pants (or closets) while they're thumping Jesus's diaries. Across the aisle the Left wants us all to get along, rescue puppies, and just be *good humans*—that is, until their disdain for so-called ignorance kicks in. A prominent liberal host said she wouldn't interview Melania Trump because she can "barely speak English." So much for the compassion of the progressives—and this woman does charity work for African nations, for Christ's sake. "Can barely speak English"—first of all, that's a fucking cop-out. If you don't like her, just admit it, but don't come up with some lame excuse. We've all heard her speak—it's not that bad. Second, you just shit on your own credibility for being a "one love, one world" supporter. The Left loves to talk about change, but they never allow people the time to accept and embrace change, nor do they have any tolerance for any opinion other than their own.

Then they wonder why people call them "elitist" and have an adverse idea about what "educated" means. Yeah, the Left can be a bunch of pretentious fucking cunts. Quote me on that. No, please. I actually enjoy watching armchair analysts spew bullshit like a fountain outside Disney World. The truth of the matter is that America is made up of regions all recycling the same retread info that their fathers, mothers, uncles, and anyone else fed them for generations. Most Americans are genetically superstitious of anything outside their comfort zone. I get it: there's safety in regurgitated mythos. However, when all you're doing is continuing the same fucking cycles of misinformation, you might as well live in a fucking hut in the woods, the good your advice is doing anyone. You're all becoming fucking farmers from Romania, digging up family members and cutting their heads off because in 2017 you still believe in vampires. You are becoming ghouls, sifting through your own feces and looking over your shoulders on the grassy knoll. Most of these people are the same ones who scream about back-alley abortions when the GOP hits the Oval Office or yell themselves hoarse that "THEY'RE COMING FOR OUR GUNS" when the Dems win. Seriously, you all need to stop that shit. It's fucking ridiculous. Nobody's taking our fucking guns. Nobody's going to truly take away your right to choice. You are becoming unpaid workers for the rhetoric arms of both parties. Knock it the fuck off.

It's a confusing time, to be honest. We live in a time when "President" Trump tried to use an executive order to ban Muslims from entering the country, only to be overturned by a federal judge, who granted a stay on prohibiting the ban because "the government hasn't thought this through." The order was rushed out so quickly that the Department of Homeland Security claimed they didn't have anything set in place to handle that sort of decree, leaving hundreds of refugees and temporary and permanent residents stranded or detained by Customs agents. Never mind that a ban like that is fucking pointless when you take into consideration that white extremists have killed more Americans than Muslim jihadists since 9/11. All this ensures that the war on terror has no end. Meanwhile the war on drugs—remember that?—only empowers the drug cartels.

And so it goes. Before you get too upset, you have to remember something: these names and phrases are simply a part of the game. Every election has its collection of buzzwords, the shit to get the constituents wound up and energized. In the seventies it was "unemployment," "gas shortages," "inflation," and so on. In the eighties it was "balancing the budget," the "war on drugs," "pro-life," and so forth. The nineties gave us "no new taxes." The 2000s gave us the "war on terror." Some of these terms have evolved, like "women's rights" and such, but the new additions are "same-sex marriage" and "healthcare," although these days they have gone rogue and made the buzzwords quite personal: his tax returns, her emails, his misogyny, her scorn and coldness. It's a dance for supremacy and likeability, because let's face it: we have no idea just how qualified these people really are. HRC could've sucked. The Cheeto might turn out to be decent from a fiscal point of view. But there's no real proof; there's just "he said, she said" until it's time to put up or shut up. This is America—we have a competitive tickling league, after all. Yeah, you read that right: a competitive tickling league.

Look it up . . .

(Everyone, please put on your Big-Person Grownup Sarcasm Goggles now. And . . . *begin* . . .)

This is going to be a contentious four years for Trump. Being a "bigly winner" really does come with having his detractors. People went as far as comparing his Inauguration Day crowds to Obama's. To be fair, Obama's crowd certainly did appear to be bigger than the Cheeto's crowd. But it was pointed out online that the reason for this was because the good people who voted for Trump "actually work for a living"! That would imply that all the people who voted for Obama are just welfare cases! HAHAHAHAHAHAHAHAHAHA, IT'S FUNNY BECAUSE BLACK AND BROWN PEOPLE DON'T HAVE JOBS!!! HAHAHAHAHAHAHAHAHAHA, IT'S A RACIST STEREOTYPE THAT ALSO PROVES THAT TRUMP WASN'T ELECTED BECAUSE OF RACISM!!! HAHAHAHAHAHA, IT ALSO DEFLATES THE WHOLE ARGUMENT THAT OBAMA ONLY HELPED PEOPLE OF COLOR GET JOBS

AND NOT GOOD CHRISTIAN WHITE FOLKS! HAHAHAHAHA-HAHAHAHAH!! THAT MAKES SENSE, RIGHT?

(You may now remove your Big Person Grownup Sarcasm Goggles until the next said portion of the book. Thank you for complying.)

Just when I think I can sit right here in the middle, get comfy in the center, avoid all the muckety-muck that is being hustled and fucked by these zealots on the outside circle, I catch myself getting more and more incensed and hurling my whole body back into the fray like Belushi in *Animal House*, punching and kicking and running on heads, *Matrix* style. I just cannot wrap my head around how this place got *so* fucking bass-ackward and blown into smithereens. Were we *always* like this? Were we *always* the biggest hypocrites in the room internationally? I realize most powerful countries or regimes dabble in globalism and slowly descend into despotism, but I always thought we had enough checks and balances inherent in our system to stop that from happening. Was I wrong? There's nothing more abhorrent than the smiling savior, languidly strolling into your comfort zone in the guise of a friend and protector and then destroying your life forever. I know this country isn't perfect—never was—but I know for a fact that even when considering the circumstances under which it was created and the unbelievable double standards that sprang as a result, this country still struggles to give its people what no other country *ever* has: the right to live and love as a *free human being*. No chains of conquest will strap you to a god or a church. No lies or malice will keep you imprisoned while you scream innocence. No law, rule, decree, order, or regulation will make it unlawful for you to breathe in the skin you're in, love whomever you want, or be whatever you want to be.

These Trump supporters go on and on about how they hate "snowflakes" and "social justice warriors" (SJWs) and all that shit when they've conveniently forgotten that our forefathers were the original SJWs. They escaped persecution over religion and authoritarianism to go to a new land where anything was possible. They then stood like a stone against tyranny and indecent behavior while a king tried to take them to task. Eventually they fought like wolves against unwelcome taxation and the trampling of personal freedoms. So the Founding Fathers railed against *all* the things that the so-called ignorant libtards also fight against. Granted, our generation tends to protest a little *too* fucking much, but I don't want to keep harping on that shit—we are still simply carrying on a tradition of agitation through demonstration. It's our rights as Americans. Without it, we'd just be the other British colony next to Canada.

Our Founding Fathers wrote the Constitution specifically to be a living document, to be amended but *never* backtracking on its core values. They did all this because they knew they would need to fix some shit later on—the overt masculinity in the paperwork and the "slavery" exception being the biggest examples of how they made some sacrifices just to get things going. Sure, it wasn't perfect. It might've gotten off to a less-than-auspicious start. But they started *somewhere.* The Constitution of the United States of America is one of the most comprehensive government documents *ever* committed to wood pulp (or, in its case, *hemp,* ironically). Most Americans only *really* know about the First and Second Amendments because those are the ones that get debated and paraphrased like crazy. I have a sneaking suspicion *most* Americans have *no* idea what the actual writing guarantees in the way of our rights. Then again, if most politicians took the time to brush up on the shit they're supposed to be upholding, they'd realize a lot of the shit they'd like to pass into law is unconstitutional—and that's on BOTH SIDES OF THE FUCKING AISLE.

I have a solution, and I know some people are going to get pissed off by it, but fuck it: it makes me laugh my balls off every time I think about it. I think the Constitution should be completely reformatted . . . with pictures. I think if the Constitution had pictures, more people would know what our rights are and more people would understand each other better. Oh, or maybe if we just changed the way it looks without changing what it means or says, we could get people to understand it. We could set it up like a video game—it does have twenty-seven amendments, so we could use those like levels! The first ten, you fight as Bill, collecting all your rights and kickboxing against the Preambles on your way to each level's big Boss. This would also help ensure that everyone who plays the game would understand how each amendment functions and how you can implement it into your lives as well. This would be fucking *awesome*. We could call it . . . 'Murica.

Level 1's Boss would try to silence Bill, or rip his mouth and heart out. To defeat the Boss, you'd have to have faith in your ability to gather people around you to help stop the Boss. The louder the voices, the weaker Boss gets, until the people shouted him or her down. Level 2 is very simple: find a gun and protect yourself from the Boss, who wants to oppress you. Level 3 and 4 would be combined: you must sneak up on this Boss, so you go from house to house, asking for room and board for the night. All the while the Boss's Preambles are searching each house illegally, trying to find you. Like a shell game, you'd move from house to house until you're able to rally enough support to pull the Boss down from the government. Level 5 would be a bit cerebral: there are several people moving around who look like you, and you must make your way through the level without giving away your intentions to the Boss's spies, who are trying to ascertain which one of you is the *real* you. So the game would go: on Level 13, you would free the Boss's slaves. On Level 22 you have to keep the other Bosses from coming back and trying to be a Boss again. Once you get to Level 27 you have the right to start over or just move through the past levels as a spectator—the borders are all open to you now, so you can go wherever you want.

Do you think that's too cheesy? Could be. I don't know—I've seen some pretty crazy shit in my time to suggest that maybe something like *that* would get us all back on the same page or, at least, the same book. I truly believe that one of the problems we have when trying to communicate with each other in this country is that no one really knows what our rights are as citizens in the greatest country around. Sure, some do. Most would like to believe they have a general idea. But the gist doesn't get it through the thick skulls of radicals and racists. In fact, they *love* it when we're all scattered because they can then feed you misinformation—"fake news"—and tell you to question the things that are actually documented and true. Some people spend their whole lives trying to ensure that we all have the right idea and the rights to *have* those ideas. Unfortunately, history has shown the good that a man or woman does in his or her lifetime almost always dies when they do—very rarely does it live past their end. That's because the zeal and energy that a single person feels for something can never truly be shared; it almost always diminishes as it passes from one person to another. In some cases that's a good thing—it means that most racist or fascist leaders are replaced by people who never feel as strongly in their resolve as the original did. It also means that people who sweat and toil for years producing refuge for people who need help are nearly always replaced by opportunists after they die. Such is the cycle of energy; it can never be duplicated emotionally. In a world where the privileged feel oppressed and children die because of petty fear, it's amazing that any of us manage to get out of bed in the mornings. Obviously, being American makes that much easier. We quite simply are the purveyors of the fruit, hanging out in Babylon's gardens, trying to do something useful with all this freedom. Some days are better than others, but you can also say that about people. The sentinels have been lackadaisical for going on, well, forever, really. But the American spirit burns. You know why we'll never get rid of war? Because we're always spoiling for a fight. That's why hippies and peaceniks are just as violent and temperamental as Nazis and thugs. To borrow a tiny bit of a phrase from the mighty Zodiac Mindwarp: "We love the fever pitch, bitch."

The next few years are going to be a bit tense, this is true. But they are also going to make us better. We will all have a better understanding of each other's lives and what it takes to be *us* when it all comes down to it. In the end we'll know where we all stand on a lot of different things. I hope that no matter what, we'll all be standing together. Now, that may seem a bit wishy-washy for some of you. That doesn't matter—I'll bet that most of you feel the same way I do deep down in your red-white-and-blue hearts. I'd be willing to bet the world on it. God knows I've lost more on less, but this one brings out the odds in me, and I've always loved being a betting man. The weight of the free world is going to be on all of our shoulders very soon. With enough backs, we'll spread the tonnage evenly.

We can take it.

We're American.

Pot it, motherfucker.

CHAPTER 4

THE KILLING NAME

IN THIS COUNTRY WE HAVE ALL GROWN UP WITH CERTAIN apocryphal situations passed down through generations, bordering on archetypical at this point. If you've ever read a book, watched a TV show, told a joke, or even come out of a cave for, like, ten fucking seconds in this country, you'll recognize the kind of stories I mean right away: the farmer and his daughters, the UFO sighting in the suburbs, the "foreign" new guy at the job and the various mishaps that come from the language barriers, the black guy in the white family's home, the white guy in the black movie theater, and so on and so forth. At this point in our lives these stories are basically the new versions of Aesop's fables or the brothers Grimm. Essentially starting out as a way to embrace our differences, these myths slowly became a way to marginalize them, making any understanding or comprehension comical and lazy. Now we don't remember the realness, just the rumor. There is no more humanity, just humor. People have stopped getting to know the others and now rely *only* on whatever they can remember from a joke. So what does this mean?

Black people are a joke. White people are a joke. Farmers are a joke. Foreigners are a joke. You can continue to take that as far as you want; it won't change anything. Now, I'm not saying you shouldn't be able to joke about people or cultures or idiosyncrasies—far from it; no one should be immune from satire and self-realization. What I *am* saying is we can't forget that everyone is different from the origins of the stereotype. Not everyone is a stereotype, no matter how easy it is to treat people as such. It's the same reason why there are no *real* universal rules of health—there are no *real* universal ways to treat other people, regardless of color or creed, race or religion, culture or stream for the mainline. Unfortunately, America has stopped putting in the work to try to get to know its people from state to state. Everyone is a fucking polling point now, a demographic, a mob to be seen for the scene. No one is allowed to be him or herself; everyone is encouraged to be one in a million, just one more piece of the crowd—because crowds can be controlled.

I'd love to see a day when we set fire to all that shit. Like, why can't we have a story about a UFO landing in the ghetto? Why can't we hear the one about the farmer who turns his neighbor on to Run DMC? Why aren't we using our imagination for something other than keeping motherfuckers in their goddamn places like a bunch of mediocre placeholders? And more importantly, why is the greatest country in the world encouraging us all to do that kind of shit? I'll tell you why: it makes us malleable, easier to manage, and quicker to herd into voting booths, strictly on a lie and a scare tactic. Fear the scary black men and Muslims—they want to kill all the crackers. Fear all the white men and Latinos—they want to kill all the blacks and burn the Bronx. Suddenly those jokes that we all laughed at become some truthful shit we all heard from a guy, and that's why we need to put so-and-so in the White House—to protect ourselves! That's how you get a nation of millions to decide against their better judgment and vote for a man the same shade as an Orange Julius.

We are four chapters in, and I guess I should have warned you: this is not my funny way of saying I hate you. There's no "wink wink" in my screaming. This is some real shit. This *could* be the angriest book I've ever written and will ever write. In fact, if I get to write another book, I'll be very surprised. But this is some shit that *needs* to be said. Why? Because you're all saying it behind each other's back and not *to* each other. The only things you reserve for each other are protests and yelling shit. I didn't want this to be spiteful, and granted, there will be moments of levity here and there. But make no mistake my friends: this isn't really a referendum; this is a fucking war horn, blasting you awake in the middle of the night from my version of Ecto-1. To arms, motherfuckers. To quote one of my favorite David Bowie lyrics, "It's in the whites of my eyes."

Before you go rooting for your own team, don't get ahead of yourselves. You forget: I *hate everyone*. I think you're all fucked in the head. If you weren't, we wouldn't be here, you wouldn't be there, and I wouldn't be writing this book. You're all fucking savages with pitchforks. Trumpers are screaming, "Get over it! You lost! He *is* your president, and you have to deal with it now! Oh and by the way, *nothing* he does is offensive—NOPE! NO NO NO NO NO! We refuse to believe it!" Meanwhile everyone else is saying, "We march! At a moment's notice, we march! Even if we are getting our way, we march! And if you disagree with our reasons, which indeed could be misinformed, we will maliciously label you a NAZI COMMIE FASCIST BIGOT NEOFANATICAL HOMOPHOBIC COCKSUCKER—while we claim 'One Love' and 'Peace' and all that shit!" This is some shit you'd hear on the playground in *elementary* school, not even junior high! What, are you all fucking five? Take your toys, go home, and let other people talk for once.

I'm not saying there aren't reasons to protest. I'm saying that when the bigger shit happens, it might be that no one is listening anymore. When a guitar is feeding back like mad, you don't stick your head in the fucking speaker; you find a way to make it stop or you leave the room. But all these fuckers defending Trump need to stop being so fucking indignant and realize that he *is* up to sheisty shit. The last time I checked, an American president shouldn't be using executive orders to ban travel on countries who've posed ZERO FUCKING THREAT to the United States while also rolling back important regulations that not only put pressure on small businesses and simultaneously ease taxes on big corporations (contrary to what he said while he was campaigning) but also make it legal for tax-exempt bodies like organized religious groups to become more politically involved. I'm not sure how up on American constitutional law you are, but that's in direct violation of the separation of church and state. It's also the reason we had the Johnson Amendment in the first place: churches shouldn't be able to regulate taste. You want to talk faith? Fine. However, your doctrine is based on some shit that came out thousands of years ago—I don't need you reinstating "cobbling" in the twenty-first century just because you're uncomfortable with modern ideas like abortion and same-sex marriage.

We're getting into that territory again, sadly. I just made sweeping statements about different groups based on conjecture and hearsay. I'm just as guilty as you are for this shit. I don't want to be, which, I guess, is why I'm writing this book—to solve some issues, to right some wrongs, to figure things out, to make peace with my own inherent bigotry and prejudice, and so on. In complicated times, why do we turn away from real complex ideas and alternatives? Why do we always go with the safest and yet most dangerously hurtful solutions? Listen, I had just as good a chance as any to grow up way different from how I am now, which is to say I could have grown up exactly how most people would have expected me to grow up, considering my background, surroundings, and family. I might've been a statistic rather than a metaphor. I could've been a liability rather than a possibility. So I understand and embrace the concept of shuffling the restraints of human hyperbole and psychosocial behavior. We can't move forward if we refuse to see each other as individual stories, instead of whole volumes of the same ol' books. If we're truly evolving genetically, then spiritually and empathetically we need to do so as well.

I think I'll tell you about Sauce Man now.

Many eons ago, before my success with Slipknot and Stone Sour, before my crazy weird adventures at the Adult Emporium, I was Corey Taylor: duly anointed taco/burrito creator at a really awesome fast-food joint called Taco Time. It was in the parking lot of Southridge Mall (back in the days when there were stores there and people actually *went* there), nestled in between a place called Golf Galaxy and O'Reilly's Auto Parts. Yeah, needless to say, it was a bitchin' place to be on a Saturday night, when everyone else was out doing really cool shit. But honestly, it was a really good gig—my bosses were a great couple who'd bought into the franchise, the people I worked with were super-cool and of various ages, and the food was FUCKING RIGHTEOUS. To this day I can't think about their crispy chicken burritos without getting a serious food boner through unforgiving denim. So even though it was "lowly fast food" and I reeked of cilantro and hamburger every night, I enjoyed it for the company and the calories I was piling on. The place was so good that it not only had the usual people ready for the quick fast-food in-and-out (no pun intended), but it also had regulars who came in every day, right around the same time. There are several who come to mind, but the one who sticks out the most is "Sauce Man."

I believe his name was Joe, but even if it wasn't, I'd probably change it anyway, so we'll just use that for now. Sauce Man was Joe, a middle-aged guy who worked somewhere in the mall during the day. Like clockwork, every day for lunch Joe would stop by, order the same pile of awesome tacos, sit down, and then slowly but surely walk from table to table, checking each bottle of Taco Time hot sauce to find the one that had the most sauce in it. Never mind the fact that I could at any moment just fill one up and give it to him—it was all part of the ritual for Joe. Then again, I could relate: Taco Time had a unique sauce with a proprietary recipe unknown even to the people who worked there. So Joe's crazy fixation was understandable. He was always kind of withdrawn and nerdy, so it took a while to get him to open up to us, but when he did, we let him know that we'd dubbed him Sauce Man. He loved it—really took to it too. He'd come in, we'd all yell, "SAUCE MAN!" and he'd smile real big and say the same thing every time: "I know, I know, I have an obsession. It's unhealthy!" For someone who looked like he could get very lonely, this seemed like it made his day.

Cut to the day I absolutely bummed him out.

I was working largely by myself, and it had turned into a really bad day. When I say "really bad day," I mean a seriously cunty, fucked-up, evil-cocksucker of a day. I was having the kind of day that makes men go rogue and overthrow governments, you understand me? I was hell in a uniform, the devil on duty. I didn't want to be there, I didn't want to work, I didn't want to talk, I didn't want to smile, and I didn't even want to *try* to do any one of those things. But because I was, I decided I was going to make it difficult for the entire world. I was pissing off customers and co-workers alike with my vocal venom. Enter Sauce Man, who came bouncing in with his usual grin and good feelings, like he'd finally gotten to the best part of his day. He strolled to the counter giving over his "I know, I know, it's a condition . . ." shtick, and like the pure prick bastard I was being, I shit all over his enthusiasm, ringing him up with little banter, making his food half-assed, and giving it to him with a nod. The pièce de résistance came when he asked me for more sauce, and I very bluntly answered with, "There's plenty on the fucking tables—help yourself" and walked into the back room, leaving poor Joe standing there with a sad and confused look on his face. When I came back out to the counter he wasn't even in the restaurant. Sauce Man grabbed some sauce, his tacos, and split. It didn't occur to me till later that maybe—*just* maybe—it was my fault he was bummed out and bailed. When I *did* put it together, I felt so fucking horrible that I swore that I'd make it right.

It took a while, though. Joe didn't come in for a while, and when he did, he was sullen and introverted again. It took a long time to get him to loosen up again, but even when he did, he was never the same around me. Maybe I'd reminded him of all the shit he'd had to go through outside the walls of Taco Time, where real life and pressures and bullshit made him feel like he was being beaten with a hose behind a bike shed. It didn't matter if I was sorry, and it didn't matter if he knew I was sorry—that fun, cool place he enjoyed had been violated by the real world. In that instant his food lost its flavor, his laugh lost its luster, and his life hit another wall. In that instant he stopped being Sauce

Man forever. Yeah, I wish that story had a happier ending. I wish I hadn't been a crabby dick stain to him. Wherever he is, I wish Joe well, and I hope the Sauce Man is raging for it at another Taco Time. I know this is a very strange parable for what I was trying to say, and at the end of the day my attitude shouldn't have any bearing on someone else's day or life. However, I'm an incredibly empathetic person—I always have been. When I don't have my head up my ass, I can usually vibe on what people are feeling.

The same goes for the rest of the world, but mainly America. We should be super-tight with each other not because of our similarities but because of our differences. We should be bulletproof just for the fact that this many different people are proud to be American and are willing to not only stand up for it but to stand together for it as well, despite the vast miles and cultural divides. How is that *not* something to aspire to? How is it *not* the very ideal we should be living up to? How can that be worse than everyone being in their own regions all sectioned off and miserable? This is the United States of America, and no matter what our government does or fucks with for our foreign policy, we should be steely and resilient in the face of that, banding together to guarantee a better day for all of us. I know that's anathema compared to how the various political parties would rather handle shit, but it's true. If we could stop communicating using only those buzzwords and filibuster, if we could get on the same page together, those pricks in Washington and the fucking White House would have to read *our* book and stick to *our* stories. But as long as we let them keep us cut up and broken down, we'll always be at their beck and call, under thumbs and overwritten.

That's why when you try to talk to someone who's a bit more conservative about certain programs that seek to help those who have little or no way to help themselves, the Republicans immediately draw blood on your conversation by throwing at you words and phrases like "welfare," "lazy," "tax drain," and whatnot. Same with the left: the minute you begin talking intelligently to a liberal about the Second Amendment and how it benefits all of us, the Democrats all start yelling "gun control," "school shootings," "dead children," and so on. And when you immediately siphon all the humanity from the conversation, it becomes a screaming match. Also, they retain control of the way you *think*. When we can no longer see how these concepts can help each and every one of us, what's the point of even having healthy discussions? Should we just all assume that the politicians would do what's right for us? Are you comfortable with a group largely composed of white males telling you what you can and can't do? Let's hope not, because that's essentially what is happening in the Cheeto's administration. We've come so far now that it's hard to imagine just how far behind the professionals would like us to return. Is apathy the new black? Will America's flag go from red white and blue to gray, gray, and gray? Will we suck the heat from the sun just to prove that it can be done?

That's not even including the violence we've seen lately.

I'm not talking about the protests. I'm talking about an elderly Trump supporter being dragged from his car and beaten until he couldn't walk. I'm talking about Muslims being ambushed so the attackers can rip their hijabs off, simply because they can. I'm talking about angry men screaming threateningly into women's faces because they're so insecure they can't handle the thought of equal anything for women. No matter how civilized or loquacious we can be or perceive ourselves to be, once we are triggered, our basest rages take a hold of us, like a police officer commandeering a car, and it strangles all common sense until all that is left is T-1000, rambling forward to kill, kill, kill, baby. I guess that's just how we do things, though. We represent an incredibly violent country; even our peace is violently maintained. The social collisions of our past might make us feel like we're advancing, but the truth is that it's all static on the screen, the big bang theory and the beginning of the universe. We collude and crash between bouts of passivity, running reds, and belching into parking spots, all in a mad attempt at *seeming* like nothing's wrong. Nothing's wrong—that is, until the spark. You know what I'm talking about: America feels like a ticking time bomb every twenty years or so. Circumstances swirl around us, backing us into cornered situations that have no good solutions. When that happens, the spark ignites, and the shit hits the fucking fan.

Civil rights, police brutality, fascist maneuvering, unemployment, injustice, reckless endangerment, unfair treatments—all these things will spit whiskey on the spark and set the world ablaze. Passion will always sway the brain when someone feels controlled and dictated to. Passion is the gas in the mob; anger is the nitrous oxide ready to blow when the shooting starts. Years ago we lit the fuse and ran for it, scattering like cigarette ash on the wind and looking for a safe place to hide. Some of us are lucky: we ghost in and out of the carnage like spectators at the coliseum, casually gazing on gladiators killing one another for the love of a mob. The rest of the world is not so lucky. While white management takes notes, everyone on the kill floor is ducking and weaving, just trying to make it through another twenty-four hours without losing their jobs, their homes, their kids, and, sometimes, their lives. This isn't visitation rights; this is "Wipeout" played inside the guts of a clock, doing your best to avoid being mulched like a pile of fucking wet leaves. That's what most people's lives are like inside the heat of the fires of freedom, just trying to cool things down so you can get some sleep at night because you know you're going to have to do it ALL OVER AGAIN TOMORROW. When you can wander in and out of "The Struggle," of course you don't realize just how dire the circumstances can become. But those who break their hands against the walls of oppression know all too well what is really going on, and I wouldn't be surprised if the lifers were more than a little resentful of the weekend warriors sometimes.

I haven't even started on religion yet.

Yes, we're going to talk about religion. Yes, I know I've gone on record as making my "peace" with many of the various religions out there. Yes, I agree if I start in on religion, it will make me look like a massive wilting double-dipping prick. But because we're on the subject and because I feel like we *might* all be friends here (except for those poor souls who bought this book thinking it was some Pro-MAGA bullshit—in that case, sucks to be you), I want you to take a deep breath . . . deeper . . . no, don't *hold* the motherfucker—I just want you to fucking relax . . . no, goddamn it, put the Vicks down, we're not huffing Vicks, we're relaxing. Now, you—*no*, we're *not* huffing *cookie dough* either! For fuck's sake, man! Now, just take a breath. Let it out. Take another. Feel better? Settled? Okay, now remind me that I might come off like a hypocrite if I take back the treaty I have with religion. Now do me favor—and this is important—ASK ME IF I GIVE A SHIT. I believe the retort you'll receive will sound a lot like the current administration.

Every corner and coast of this country had its own sort of religion and about a thousand fucking offshoots: Mormon, Baptist, Christian, Catholic, Scientologist, Presbyterian, Moony, Jew, Jehovah's Witness, Seventh Day Adventist, Quaker, Puritan, Amish, Samaritan, and every fucking fractured faction in between. They are all screaming "Faith!," they are all ready to absolve you of your sins if you believe, and most of all, they all fucking hate each other. They dog each other's doctrines, they slag the other's ideas about peace, and they do whatever they can to be the Big Cult on Campus. That's all that these fucking houses are, you know: they're just fucking cults. Sure, they have better PR and packaging, but don't let the leather couches and commercial breaks fool you: the only difference between the Moonies and the Mormons is the neighborhoods they rule over. Sure, you can make the case that I'm talking about Organized Religion, not religion. I assure you, though, these days there is very little difference. They all subtly encourage fanatical behavior, they all preach that their way is the only true way to whatever name their version of "heaven" goes by, and they all teach distrust for anyone who doesn't believe what they believe, leading to constant conflict and controversy.

Is that what happens when something comes to America and becomes infected with "democracy" or "capitalism"? Does something like religion become overly severe and overtly diabolical when it's exposed to a free market and tax exemption? I've long said that just as the United States can take a good idea and make it incredible, it would stand to reason that it can also take a horrible idea and turn it into a cultural epidemic. We seem to have a way of juicing the shit out of the most stringent concepts; everyone and everything we know is on some sort of booster, so why not our states of mind? Could this explain why we're so ready to tear each other's throats out over stupid fucking boycotts like Starbucks and Budweiser? Don't get me wrong: I think it's fucking hilarious when hard cases on both sides of shitty arguments try to kill each other. I love listening to and watching rabid followers of rhetoric and "alternative facts" attack while also being attacked. It's like being in the audience for a full-contact, no-holds-barred version of "I know you are, but what am I?" complete with chainsaws, baseball bats, and cream pies loaded with that crazy evil acid shit from *Killer Klowns from Outer Space*. As much as it drives me fucking banana sandwich, I could read the exchanges online all fucking day—it's ridiculous, misspelled, and almost always dangerous. If it's not liberals threatening to set fire to places that don't acquiesce to what they find "progressive and fair," then it's bigoted conservatives sending out cartoons of racially stereotypical scapegoats being shot in the head. Yes, it's fucking madness. However, who's going to stop it? The president? In one day—ONE FUCKING DAY—he denounced the Dakota Access Pipeline protesters, saying it wasn't even controversial because "he hadn't heard anything about it." *And* he offered to ruin the career of a senator from Texas because he wouldn't play ball with law enforcement's hopes to deregulate certain civil seizure laws. Yeah, the Cheeto is *really* known for his kind-heartedness and open spirit . . .

You've got to remember—it's me. I don't care what the fuck some of you do to each other. I know I spoke about empathy a little bit ago, but you motherfuckers are pushing me to the edge of my usually even-keeled temper. No, that's not right—I *do* have a temper. So what the hell am I talking about? Oh yeah, my psychotically gnarly imagination. Let me start again: you motherfuckers are pushing me to indulge my psychotically gnarly imagination. This country has become a schoolyard full of petulant bullies screaming with their fingers in their own ears, and what's worse is that the orange principal is trying to arm the faculty to kill everyone. I'm just the hall monitor trying to get out of the school before the ovens explode. I wasn't sure if it was going to get better or worse, but I feel like this shit would be happening even if HRC had won both the popular vote *and* the Electoral

College. That's how much we all hate each other, honestly for no really good fucking reason.

It feels like a nostalgic resurgence of the tensions of old: the Cold War, Uncle Tom, Jim Crow, putting the "Ms." in misogyny . . . I mean, I *guess* it stands to reason. As far as the zeitgeist goes, we tend to see fashion and fads fold back on themselves every twenty years, so it would make a bit of sense to realize maybe the same thing happens with agitation and unrest. Do people get uncomfortable with comfort, and if so, is it a specifically American thing that comes with the safe space of freedom and choice? Do we get so blasé about stability that we let ourselves slip into antiquated discontent? The alternative is a little scarier: we're all a mish-mash of bastards and bitches who will never get along and would rather burn each other's houses down. If I had on my Big Person Grownup Sarcasm Goggles on, I'd look at it this way: WHEEEEEEEEE!!!!! WE'RE ALL GOING TO DIE!!!! HAHA-HAHAHA, IT'S FUNNY BECAUSE IT'S STUPID!!!! I CAN'T WAIT TO NOT BE FUCKING STUPID!!!! WHEN WILL THAT BE, UNCLE FUCKMOUTH!?

That's a great fucking question . . .

In early 1992 I had moved back to Waterloo, Iowa, to live with my mom for a while. Things had gotten a little hot for me in Des Moines, and I needed to duck down and lay low as things cooled off. Don't ask what possessed me to move back to 319—I didn't have a lot of money, and my choices were slim and shit. So I went back to where I'd sworn I'd never go again: the scene of so much pain and abuse and the setting of every sun I'd said goodbye to. I moved in with my mom and got a job roofing and siding with her ex-boyfriend. And for four months that was all I did. I didn't play music, I didn't write, and I didn't have a future. I drank, crawled through my bedroom window, passed out, woke up, went to work, and repeated. I wasn't sure what I was going to do with my life, but what worried me the most was: What if this was *all* I was going to do with my life? What if I'd let all that potential go to shit?

Overnight shit changed.

Waterloo has always been a racially diverse city, so much so that most people have referred to it as "Little Detroit." This, of course, comes with its own dose of tensions, which, in 1992, the riots in response to the verdict in the Rodney King police brutality trial exacerbated. After *not one* officer was found guilty, even with video proof, Los Angeles erupted into chaos and flames, violence and mayhem, and an unrequited need for vengeance. From the courthouse that sense of injustice ran rampant through the streets of South Central and beyond, like the Flash with a blowtorch and gasoline. Block by block, building by building, the victims exacted what they needed to relieve this pressure, even as they burned their own businesses and neighborhoods. This is what indifference does to people: they will destroy their own dreams for all to see to make sure the guilty cannot sleep at night. For those of us who are old enough to remember watching this live, it was a frightening vision of the future. Only a racist cunt would've wished for those cops to be set free. But at some point we'd have to look outside our own doors. That sense of hurt and anger had spread across the country. Chicago, Detroit, New York, Atlanta, New Orleans, you name it—it was happening. Not on the same scale as LA, mind you, but the fire was definitely spreading. Waterloo, Iowa, was no exception.

I was sitting in a car with a friend at 2 A.M. on the night of the Rodney King riots. We'd both had the night off, and we decided to go out and "cruise Uni"—essentially drive up and down University Avenue, looking for girls and kicks. After a fruitless search we both agreed it was time to chill and crash, so we were driving back from Cedar Falls (where Uni ends) to my friend's house in Evansdale, not far from my mom's old place off of Butler in Waterloo. It was quiet; the only thing we could hear was the radio. We were both pretty smoked, so we weren't talking, just riding along, looking forward to some shuteye. We pulled up to a light right at the end of University, where it used to split and turn into a street that I can't remember the name of right now. It was a dark corner, not a lot of houses or anything, just a couple of empty lots and one abandoned building that used to be a BBQ restaurant. The light was red; the street was quiet.

Like something out of a movie, that changed in an instant.

We missed how it started, but the parking lot in front of that BBQ joint had begun to fill with a crowd of probably thirty or forty black people—standing, talking, slowly starting to shout and yell. They were incensed and enraged, and with good fucking reason. They'd just watched justice get fucked in the ass on live TV. They'd also watched their black brothers and sisters say, "fuck civility" and go to town on a world that thought it was okay to allow that kind of unchecked aggression go unpunished. So they gathered together to talk, then to unite, then to channel all that pain into some type of release. They were just in the midst of a rallying cry with several fists in the air when they became very aware of the two white boys sitting at the stoplight by themselves watching all this unfold. With a silent malice they *all* turned toward us . . . and began walking slowly toward the car, as if to surround it.

Now, before I go any further, I am *not* telling you this story to compel some sort of hateful response toward the crowd. Yes, at the time I was so fucking scared that I was shitting pairs of pants I wasn't even wearing at the time. But even after it was all said and done, I never blamed anybody for anything, and I certainly didn't use it as an excuse to tap into some hidden racist agenda on my part. It may have freaked me out at the time, but as crazy as it sounds, I understood what was going on. You'd have to be an ignorant fool not to see why this could happen. I know what you're thinking, and you're right: I didn't come to that conclusion *in* the moment; it happened afterward. But I still never used it to validate any inner hatred. I will say I was freaking the fuck out as they began to surround the car. There was a lot of shit being screamed at us: "What are you looking at, white boy?" "Get out of the car, motherfuckers!" "Come on—we got something for you!" My friend was behind the wheel, and thank god he was—I'd spaced out just listening to all the shit they were screaming at us. He, however, had the wherewithal to hit the gas, run the red light, and get us the fuck out of there. In the rearview mirror we could see them start to give chase but then relent and give up. Neither of us spoke until we stopped at his house.

That's the kind of world we live in at times: where total strangers can become mortal enemies because of the actions of *other* total strangers trying desperately to control and manipulate others. It's been twenty-five years since that night in front of the BBQ restaurant, and I can tell you right now that I can still feel the fear in my gut from that moment when the rage boiled over out of our favor. I do *not* blame them for coming at us. If they'd gotten hold of us and fucked us up, I might harbor some sort of ill will, but I would still understand where it came from. This is why empathy is so important for our growth. This is why the future *must* have the respite we sincerely need. This is why if we can't reach deep down inside ourselves, step out of our own shoes and into a pair that belongs to someone else, we are truly damned. We will truly be on the path toward walls, bans, and mutually assured destruction—all of which will occur inside our own borders, crossing our own boundaries and scrubbing out our own lines. This place will turn into the charred remains of the Temple of Doom, bubbling over like a shaken Pepsi and spraying us all in the eyes with disdain and murder.

Sorry to be a bum-out, but it's true. These are crazy times, true believers (love you, Stan!), and in times like this a hero *must* rise to balance the scales. We have our "villain," whether the people who voted for him believe it or not. No amount of joking or trivializing or pandering or dismissing or forgiving or overlooking will cover the fact that this man wants to be our *ruler*, not the president. He wants judges to roll over for him, he wants Congress to just give in to him, and he wants us *all* to bow to him because he approaches our government like a cross between Putin and *Celebrity Apprentice*: as long as he feels like he's popular, he will try to strip us all of our rights until only the elderly rich white men have a say in matters. Game—set—strike the match, because the USA will be a fucking powder keg on that day. It feels like a vicious cycle, running from extreme to extreme, finding the love, pushing it away, embracing the hate, and sauntering by, and the world keeps turning on a knife's point, ready to pierce or be pierced. Apathy is not a good system of government; running one like a business is just as fucking stupid.

The scars from our Civil War, Griffith's *Birth of a Nation*, 1968, and every act of violence all the way up to the present day have been torn asunder, spilling blood that is red, black, white, blue, brown, and beige. If you think America is *only* white, you're a fucking coward with hate in your heart and no room to play with others. If you think this country is only white, ask the people who were here *before* us—you know, those people we gave hope to when they protested the Dakota Access Pipeline and won, then we said nothing as Trump overturned it all and made the Army Corps of Engineers fire up the drills again. I'm sure they will agree, saying, "Of *course* this country is only for whites. White people are the only ones who get any fucking justice here." I'll bet you dollars to doughnuts you'd get the same answer from blacks, Latinos, Asians, Muslims, and everyone else on the spectrum, regardless of whether they were born here.

What a boring sweet hell that would be: just a sad country full of nothing but white motherfuckers in shitty suits and horrible company. I'd rather chug bleach on national television.

Hope might be hard to come by in a state like this, but I still have it. I still have hope when there are people like Elizabeth Warren, Tom Nichols, Van Jones, Cory Booker, and a host of others who refuse to just let the despot have his way. If we can all find a way to see the truth, no matter how shitty it is, we might avoid the eviction of Eden and not have to move in next door at the Dystopia Hotel. Yeah, the rent's cheaper, but you pay a heavier price at the end of it: the hidden fees will literally kill you. We need to focus on the things we do have in common, but we also need to accept and find a way to love the things that make us the different and cool members of the USA. We belong because we love it here. We'd fight for it because we love it here. We'd all die protecting it because we love it here. Never mind the rah-rah patriotic horseshit—I'm talking about loving the cities, states, countryside, coasts, people, diversity, sunshine, snow tops, mountains, deserts, highways, byways, rivers, oceans, majesty, and majority here. Not only could this country still be the freest, but it's also one of the most beautiful. If we could only get it to be cooler, I think we'd really be on to something over here.

Grab someone's hand today and tell him or her it's going to be okay. When the turds are flying at the windmill's blades, hand out some umbrellas or do the noble thing and block some of that shit with your body. Be a hero for a stranger. Be a friend for an enemy. Be bigger and better than those little assholes. There's a way to "go high when they go low," where it doesn't feel like we rolled over and showed our bellies before we pissed in terror. There's also a way to have humanity and compassion while also lending credence to the idea that "if you *dare* to fuck with me and mine, I will most assuredly do some fucking damage to you and yours." It is not a violation of the human spirit to defend people you care about. It is not abandoning your principles when you fight for what you love. Like I said before, we are not *nearly* as evolved as we'd like to be; stop acting like a fucking hippy science fiction movie, and kick some ass for once. It feels good—really good, actually. It might even make you fuck a little better and harder at the end of the day.

Sadly, until that happens, we are left to pick up the pieces left on the playground while the accused shuffle back to class, looking for one last chance to fuck each other over before the bell rings. Make no mistakes, boys and girls: this reckoning is *going* to happen, whether we like it or not. Whether we choose to learn something—*anything*—from this experience is for you to decide. I still feel terrible for letting myself think that things were better than they were, and I think that's how it got away from us. We stopped trying to be a decent nation, and it bit us right in the dicks and grabbed us *all* by the pussies. So we allowed the uninformed to make a horrible decision that they won't truly comprehend for a very, very long time. But I also think the damage is going to head into their own backyard sooner than later, so they'll be just as fucked as the rest of us when the shit storm comes raining down on the Macy's Parade. I might need to bring you some *better* umbrellas, to be fair. But we'll see what happens.

Until then, remember:

There is war in the eyes of America, and the targets are closer to home than they've been in a long, long time. America is going to burn, and what's sad is that for the most part, it will deserve to burn.

CHAPTER 5

HILLARY, EMAILS, AND THE FALL OF THE HOUSE OF KENNEDY

LIBERALS, LOOK, SERIOUSLY, WE HAVE TO TALK.

I mean, we usually have a lot in common: we have empathy for other people (mostly) when it appears they're being oppressed, we tend to give a helping hand to those in need, we love the challenge of fighting for equal rights and freedoms for those who can't fight for themselves, and we all love to point out the hypocrisy of those shits on the other side of the aisle when they act like they're doing everything they can for people. Just like you, I am dedicated to trying to fix those misconceptions the politicians love to keep alive out there along with all the other rhetoric, like "working class" only means white people and "poor" or "poverty level" is code for minorities of any other color. Just like you, I love a good rough-up with a big, bad bully. Just like you, I despise prejudice on every level, including when it comes to the prejudices on the Left, like treating people from the South like common criminals or like they're all dumb hicks who don't know a damn thing about anything. I feel you. I'm with you, honestly. Even all you Hollywood liberals who make yourselves targets by putting yourselves out there for every opinion and accepting the fact that "common folk" are going to argue and disagree with almost every newer concept you float out into the void, like a nice, fat softball easy for the joy zone. I know you all *mean* well. I know you all *seem* like fairly intelligent cats for whom the big matters of the world and our country for the most part are very, *very* serious causes that you would give all kinds of time to if you weren't so busy. I get it—or at least I try to anyway. You truly are trying to keep everyone's best interests in mind as it pertains to the masses who need a good washin'. But, um, I have a question, one that's been bothering me for a few months. It shouldn't take long—then again, I shouldn't have to ask. That's life, I guess. So here goes.

If you're all so fucking smart about shit that makes yours not stink, then how the *fuck* did you allow the screwing of that much pooch at the *Oscars*?!

I mean, for fuck's sake, I watched that shit with a slack-jawed hopelessness that left me stunned like a catfish after the lightning hits the water. It wasn't even funny; it was Steve Harvey all fucking over again, and I thought *that* situation was a weird fucking put-on to begin with. But *this* . . . Jesus wept. Between the look on Warren Beatty's face and the painful correction that was eventually delivered by the gentleman whose name I never bothered to learn because of fucking angry reasons, no amount of rubbing my eyes was going to save me from the butt-fuckery happening on that stage. I might've let this go if it hadn't been the capper in a line of frustrating errors committed in the name of most of us progressives just trying to do what's right. Don't believe me? How about the commercial that the Hollywood Left shot imploring the head of the Electoral College to take it upon "himself" to do what was right in order to block the election of the Cheeto.

They all read from printed-out pages that stated the various legal powers granted to the head of the College, including—and I'm paraphrasing—making the decision to swing those votes toward the more just candidate. Each and every celebrity—be they actor or singer, male or female—implored with true emotion that this "man" do what was right for the country, even using "his" name, as a sign of playing like they actually knew "him."

There was only one problem with that, and it's also the reason I've been using quotes this whole time: the head of oversight for the Electoral College was, in fact, a woman. You'd *think* they would have checked on that before they shot a very expensive-looking commercial. There's haste, and then there's fucking rushing to judgment. I'm not saying that I didn't agree with what they were fucking saying, but motherfucker, you'd *better* make sure you don't look like a goddamn asshole yourself when you're trying to paint somebody else as "unfit for the job."

Yeah, yeah, yeah, before you even come at me with that shit about "liberals don't all live in Hollywood," it was a joke. That seems to be the prerequisite for being a liberal or a progressive on the Left these days: no fucking sense of humor. I'm not talking about shitty racist jokes or demeaning misogynistic anecdotes; I just mean jokes in fucking general. You can't find the humor in imperfection if you believe that you yourself are a perfect snowflake in danger of melting in the heat of truth. Then again, it *might* be the massive ego trips and elitist attitudes that have caused an entire political party and its way of thinking to be ridiculed or immediately treated with disrespectful scrutiny and disdain. That sort of reaction was usually reserved for those zealous bozos on the Right back in the days when everything they said was poison and every program they tried to push through Congress seemed to leave no one with clean water or air. Nothing's really changed, but now everyone seems suspicious of liberal points of view, like suddenly it's a sin to be successful *and* informed—when you can be, that is—*except* when it comes to their Great Orange Dick Tater. I find it amazing that Hollywood is vilified for having values in their tax bracket, and yet Trump on paper appears to be the same way, but they listen to him because he's parroting shit they think they believe instead of looking at the reality of what the Left has to offer.

I was sitting on a Southwest flight from Des Moines to Las Vegas, stuck between a young man furiously destroying imaginary battleships and an elderly guy who reeked of a 1970s casino, desperately trying to figure out why this conclusion was the case and writing it down as quickly as I could as it came to me in fits and starts (as opposed to shits and farts) when I finally hit on it. In fact, I'd already written it down. I'd figured it out a long time ago and maybe hadn't wanted to admit it too loudly because deep down in my dark asshole of a soul, I knew that occasionally I was just as guilty as the liberals in this respect. I knew it—I just needed to say it out loud: most people tend to cringe and bristle at the thought of the Left because liberals come off as pretentious, elitist, egotistical, and mean toward "normal people." It doesn't matter whether most people could agree or identify with what liberals are saying. No one—and I mean NO FUCKING ONE—wants to feel like they are being judged. No one wants to feel like the sharpest glare is being reserved for his or her viewpoint. In every region of this country there are hundreds of cultures observed by millions of Americans as diverse as the original crowds at Lollapalooza '92. We're still a melting pot. We're still an amalgam of colors, beliefs, and genders. But the fire that keeps it all boiling and bubbling is beginning to burn through the bowl, covering us all in crazy liquid plastic and white-hot rage.

It's in fact one of the main reasons I wanted to write this book in the first place. I'll quote my good buddy Stubs again: "I'm socially liberal but fiscally conservative." As I'll point out soon, I feel like most of the country is just like that. My biggest problem is that I have a hard time seeing myself in the various politicians and celebrities who purport to have the same ideals and beliefs that I do. I crave intelligence on a genetic level, but I detest the feeling of making people feel like they are ignorant. I support choice across the board, and yet I become incensed when the Left becomes just as cunty and inflexible as the Right appears to be. I want real change, but I also want change at a pace that's consistent with the state of the nation, not change that's a reflection of the pretense of the hierarchy and its casual elitism against those people who don't have the easiest access to the latest information. Even when regular people see the info and have the time to process it, they balk and don't immediately accept it because it may clash with their religious beliefs. Instead of slowing the roll and helping those people out, the cocks on the walk make them feel inferior because they "still cling to ancient gods for answers that science readily provides." These are faithful people who look to the Good Book for guidance, especially when it comes to family and life, and you just shit all over their ways; yeah, I can't *possibly* see why they would treat everything we tend to say with distrust and hate. Welcome to self-righteous reverse prejudice.

Sorry, we'll get back to that, but first let me give you an example: Sarah Palin is a fucking *moron*.

Yeah sure, in certain angles of light she looks like she might be a bit savvy and even easy on the eyes, but goodness gracious great balls of fire, she makes Barney Fife look like Sir Isaac Newton. There was a story floating around the intra-webs right around the time President Obama was presenting people with congressional medals of honor, including then Vice President Joe Biden. There were pictures showing the former POTUS with an award of his own. Breitbart, the fake news site that shills for the racist right (and also where Trump goes to masturbate over stories about himself . . . allegedly . . .), posted a news item accusing Obama of giving himself one of the congressional medals of honor. Palin, dickhead that she is, saw the story and immediately tweeted the link across Twitter, including her own simple attempts at informed contempt. When the story was debunked and she was later found to be misinformed and mistaken, she took it down but left the snark because why not? After all, she hunts fucking moose and all. Look, I know I'm in dangerous territory anyway by skirting the very line between hypocrite and hoodlum that I was talking about, but Sarah Palin is no one to look to when you want to be informed. She has no credibility, barely any grasp on decency, and, from my perspective, is officially a shit-stained asshole with bits of paper clinging to the tiny hairs she couldn't reach because she's not smart enough to know that hair grows there, and if she knows, she keeps forgetting it fucking grows back. You may not agree with me and you may not think it's funny, but I do and I don't give a shit.

You can get as assed as you want at me saying that, but seriously? After all the shit I've heard "good people" say about Obama over the years, none of which I'll fucking utter here because it pissed me off so bad that I had to leave the room, you're lucky I'm taking it easy on that club-footed mouth breather. And with that stroke of bias, I make myself just as fucking bad as all the other elitists floundering right now to prove just how right they are on the Left side of the country. I don't think it's the *only* issue they have, but it's a huge one. You can't be a party of the people if you can't relate to people in the first place. Then again, am I committing the same sin by not acknowledging the groundswell that happened during the election? Yes, Clinton II had an overwhelming majority in the popular vote. It's only because of tiny slivers of the voting public that Drumpf took the win in the first place. Seriously—look it up. He won the Rust Belt—Pennsylvania, Michigan, and Ohio—by tiny percentages. So when these asshats on the Right trot out their maps showing solid red all over the country with the exception of the blue on the coasts as a way to fuck with the "coastal elites," it gets me savage for a variety of reasons. One, some of those southern states are *very* rural, so the concentrations of the populace are misrepresented drastically. Don't believe me? Look at all the people who are *still* protesting in every town, city, state, and region. Oh, and by calling them "paid protesters," you're pissing off your *own* voters as well, Republicans. Two, touting that map as proof that there's a mandate going on is complete bullshit as well. Clinton II clearly won the popular vote, no matter what your delusional Cheeto keeps harping on. Then you need to add in all the people who wiped their asses with their ballots by voting for Johnson and Stein. *Then* you have to consider the people who just straight-up didn't vote because they weren't comfortable with *any* of the choices. That pretty much takes your "mandate" theory and pegs it in the ass with a vacuum attachment. Sorry, but you're wrong. I wouldn't be as blasé and "whatever" about the whole thing if it weren't for one simple thing: Clinton II was always described as so fucking unlikeable.

It boggles the mind. She had the stronger campaign. She had the stronger message. She had the most pop, the most momentum. She won the popular vote by the most votes in history. The only reason she's not the president right now is because she didn't get the *right* votes. Herein lies a clue to why people don't generally like her: she is the *face* of that hated liberalism the Right loves to prop up like a Halloween scarecrow for the Reagan kids to laugh at. She represents everything good and bad about liberals: intelligent (pretentious), powerful (elitist), savvy (judgmental), and kind (the benevolent snob). I'm not saying I agree with any of this. I'm telling you what the other side thinks because I have that unique perspective. It's not the various programs she wanted to champion; I feel like most Americans in any financial situation would appreciate the helping-hand initiatives she wanted to push. It comes down to what she stands for in their eyes. It has to—lower-class and working-class families have always been able to get by with some help provided by the government. So voting against their own interests *has* to come down to a real lack of likeability. I don't think Clinton II is better or worse than any of the other politicians; I just think she's a politician. She definitely had the goods to do this gig, and anyone who disagrees is probably too busy eating paste from a preschooler's desktop. You think Trump is more qualified than Hillary? That fucking mook can't even keep his Twitter in his pants at night. Fuck him.

The Hillary thing *has* to be because people just didn't like her. Anyone screaming "emails" or "Benghazi" or any other shitty campaign herring can shut the absolute fuck up right now. Clinton II didn't do *anything* with emails that both Colin Powell and former president George W. Bush didn't already do before she came into the administration. Benghazi just happened to occur on her watch, just like Yemen and Syria just happened to occur on Trump's watch. No, she may not have handled the testimony very well, but that's not fucking illegal. This whole idea that she could be put up on charges for some shit like emails is preposterous, especially when you take into consideration that Trump had a classified briefing in front of hotel guests at his shithole in Florida, not to mention the military personnel who carry the nuclear football taking pictures with guests for Instagram. And before you start bringing up dumbass conspiracy shit from Info Wars and that cunt Alex Jones, do me a favor: burn my book. You're not going to like me if you ever meet me. There was absolutely nothing that took away from Hillary's qualifications for the presidency of the United States. From my side of the fence the reasons people don't like her are thus: she's cold and calculating, she's a woman, and she served on the Obama administration. In the eyes of conservatives and the Righteous Right, that's all you really needed to fight like heathens to make sure she didn't win.

Yep, just straight-up misogyny will do for a major factor. Then you add to that the racism that rose up in response to our first black president, and it was going to be hard to get the hat trick for first female president. I know Obama wasn't perfect. I know he did just as much weird shit as any white president. But in a lot of ways that's why he's my favorite: because he proves the equality of the races in a way that can help us let go of that smug assertion that some of us are better than others because we don't *treat* people like they're better than others. Think about *that* lateral head-fuck for a second, and you'll go full-on *Scanners,* Michael Ironside style. Obama wasn't perfect—he wasn't *supposed* to be. But people were already building his mythos, much like they did with Kennedy before he died. Once Kennedy was murdered, he was deified, and all his dirty secrets were swept under rugs, then locked in vaults, waiting for the high volume of docs made in the eighties to establish that America's prince was flawed, that America's Camelot was just as fabled in real life as the original, a false front designed to fan the flames of hope no matter how vivid the truth may be. That's why I think the Eternal Flame is the most appropriate dedication to JFK—because as long as there is youth and vigor to fight the good fight, those fires will burn at home and abroad for all time.

Okay, let's get away from Hills for a split second and talk about something liberals do that drives me up fucking Mulholland and back. It kind of goes hand and hand with another aspect of being liberal that pisses me off: the lack of follow-through. Sure, the base is all electrified now that the Cheeto is rubbing his ass on everything inside the Oval Office. But before the inauguration you would've had to check these frilly Left hands for a pulse just to see if they were kicking. They were the party of all talk but no action. Seriously, that's why I had so much respect for Republicans: when they said they were going to do something, by fucking Odin, they did it, and if someone challenged them on it, they told them all to get the fuck out of their faces. That is how you get shit done. But Democrats all too often rely on the outrage of the people to shut down any criticism instead of just backing their collective shit up with attitude and intelligence. Nine times out of ten they'd never stand up for themselves; they'd always claim they were "taking the high road" or "going high when they go low." What a fucking pile of burning Goodyears. You're in fucking politics: THERE IS NO HIGH ROAD. Lose this convoluted sense of righteousness and get your hands dirty. You don't have to go full fuckface, but you *do* have to act like you have a spine. Being in the moral right does *not* mean you have to be a fucking coward.

It's this double standard when it comes to doing the right thing that has led to a sort of passive-aggressive approach to helping in the community or just plain helping others. I may catch some hell for this from some of you pseudo-peacenik neophytes, but

I have to tell you something: ideas like the "homeless gift bag" are a crock of shit. If you're not familiar with the concept of the homeless gift bag, let me enlighten you as best I can. It's a double-edged sword, this idea: there are good connotations and bad observations to be had on all sides, considering the vibe behind it in the first place. It's almost like a sort of "pay it forward" but not really. Let me explain: the idea behind the homeless gift bag is ostensibly to fill several plain, biodegradable sacks with dried goods and maybe some spare clothing or toiletries. You would then take them all over to a Thanksgiving dinner or a Christmas party, offering *the recipient* the opportunity to take these items out and give them to people in need or homeless people who haven't been able to make it to a mission or a shelter. Honestly, I have a hard time bagging on a concept like this because the end result *does* actually help people when it's done correctly. It's a wonderful gesture, and it requires just a few minutes of your day to make sure that not only do you get it done but that the people who receive it get it at its freshest or at least as soon as physically possible. Trust me, it's a really charitable idea for a worthy cause.

Now allow me to hand the microphone over to Captain Prick Biscuit . . .

This is such a lazy attempt at doing charitable work that it makes my fucking blood boil under my already thin fucking skin. For all intents and purposes, people put these homeless gift bags together because "they couldn't afford a really nice gift for everyone this year, so instead they want you to pay some good will forward." You couldn't afford a decent gift, yet you had plenty of money to spend on all these supplies? Don't get me wrong: I'd rather have you buying things like that for other people, but don't fucking lie to me like you're doing me a fuckin' favor. That's like shitting in my mouth and calling it a pudding pop. Also, if you were going to go to all that trouble to get things to hand out to homeless people, why the fuck didn't you just do it yourself? Why wouldn't you take all these dried goods and spare belongings out, pass them to the people who need them, then tell us what you did in our names? I'll fucking tell you why: because buying the shit is the *easy* part, and you can still feel self-righteous about "avoiding all the consumerism that hangs from the holidays like a hangman's noose because you did something good and nice for people"—that is, except you didn't. You didn't actually do anything nice for anyone other than yourself. I'm sure you *told* people that you did all the work because that's what most hippies do anyway: talk a great game then dump the ball off when the win is on the line. What you *actually* did was put more work on other people's plates than maybe they really have time for, like people who work multiple jobs or families full of kids. Yeah, what you did was a chicken-shit attempt at being a saint, all so you could play the martyr. You want to show me something? Next time do it yourself. I know houses where there are *still* some of those bags left over from the holidays, and *that* family also gets saddled with the guilt because it got lost in the shuffle. Not you modern-day Mother Teresas, though: your hands are clean because you washed your hands of that responsibility long ago. Fuck you very much, you cunts.

It's getting harder and harder for me to back this team with all that shit going on. It's not that I don't support the cause and the values behind it; it's that I can't stand some of the faces of the party anymore. Hell, half the time I don't even *know* who's driving the bus, you know? All I know is that the Democratic Party has a pretty spotless and spectacular fucking record for blowing the shit out of a victory, even when that victory could be considered guaranteed. During the campaign the *second* I saw the contention between the DNC and the Bernie Sanders supporters, I had an inkling they may lose this thing. Then came all the behind-the-scenes garbage where the head of the DNC basically was railroading the Sanders campaign, even though it had the groundswell *way* before "I'm With Her." That's another thing the Democrats have never gotten the hang of: street-level passion. I'm not going to sit here and say Bernie would've beaten Trump—I'm not that skilled in the dark arts of prophecy right now. But what I will say is this: if they hadn't split the foundation, the House of Kennedy would probably still be in charge. If they hadn't tried to play fast and loose with "next man up" while also sabotaging one of their brightest stars (albeit one of their oldest—and also one who only declared himself "Democrat" so he could run for president), maybe the ship would be right on target and we wouldn't have the opening to *Dawn of the Dead* going on right now. This is all based on eyewitness accounts, simple common sense, and the bigger picture, seeing as everyone I know has said the same goddamn thing to me on the subject.

Now we have a DNC led by two guys most people only heard about because all the recognizable names are on vacation. I'm not knocking their cred or their abilities, but I will say this: after Trump's speech to Congress, the Democratic rebuttal seemed like the usual liberal shoot-yourself-in-the-foot tactic. Instead of building on the momentum and passionate word on the street because of all the support and activism going on against the various policies the GOP is trying to push through, who do the fucking Democrats put out there to talk to the American people? A WHITE MALE WHO APPEARS TO BE JUST SHY OF HIS SEVENTIETH BIRTHDAY, SITTING UNDER A HOT TIN ROOF AT A 4H POTLUCK, DRESSED IN HALF A CANADIAN TUX AND ABOUT A VERB AWAY FROM WHITTLING A PIECE OF WOOD FOR HIS

GREAT-GRANDKIDS. And with that final shot, the coolness of the liberal Democratic Party passed silently in the night like a fart in a windy car, never really to be heard from again. When most of your supporters seem to be people of color and a great deal of whom are female, who in their left-handed right mind would turn the cameras on the antithesis of your base? The dude looked just like Mike fucking Pence, for god's sake! I'm not saying the guy has the same qualities as Pence—probably far from it; however, when those two *could* be mixed up in lineup, do you think you could've found a better way of saying "fuck you" to the people who've been marching and screaming since the day you let the "W" slip out of reach?

It's hard to defend this party and this point of view when the Democratic Party honestly has set themselves up for failure at every turn and opportunity. I'm convinced that Democrats only win by accident. Obama only won because it was Obama. Clinton I only won because it was Clinton. I feel like the only person to really win on the merit of the party was Carter, and even he was dragged through the mud a few hundred times before the country remembered why they loved him in the first place: because he's a good man who tries for the absolute best this country can provide for us. That's the only thing I can really think about right now; then again, maybe that's the case with *all* presidents, regardless of politics or policy. Reagan won because it was Reagan, Bush Sr. won because he'd done a great job under Reagan . . . okay, after that I have no fucking idea how the others got there. Dubya was the good ol' boy most people could relate to, and Trump is just a celebrity who got lucky. That's like saying Schwarzenegger won because of his political background—he won because he's *Ahh-nold*. Trump won because he's famous, not because of his expertise. If he were *really* that good, he'd have released his fucking taxes. Hell, he'd have plastered them all over billboards and Times Square if he weren't hiding the fact that he sucks at pretty much everything.

When I was a kid I couldn't understand why so many people got so bent out of shape over things like free school lunches or food giveaways or even musical programs in school. I'd hear the bile in the arguments, talking about how "they don't pay taxes to support poor people and their laziness" and "why the hell should I have to kick in for shit I don't feel like I should—I work too hard" and all that jazz and nonsense. They would get all huffy like they were the *only* ones paying for things like that. Now, of course, these are the very programs the Republicans are trying to get rid of, even though every day these programs help nearly all the people who voted for these guys. In a world where the people who *need* these programs largely vote for the politicians who *hate* these programs, how in the ever-lovin' hell do they have a majority in the House of Representatives and the Senate? How the *hell* did Trump win the presidency? I'll tell you why: because Democrats have never stopped trying to appeal to the intelligentsia in this country, the Snob Squad. Even though their values are more in line with the greater public than the Republicans are, the Dems only really care about going for the "cooler" crowd. That's no shock: that goes back to when Joe Kennedy was running his son John's campaigns all over the Eastern seaboard. It also smacks right in the face of that elitism that turns us all off. It'd be like a really great rock 'n' roll band deciding they *only* want to appeal to the man-bun and beard crowd in Silver Lake, a suburb of Los Angeles. There *are* worse fates than that, but not fucking many of them, I'm telling you right now.

Let me be frank and earnest with you (although I will not answer to "Frank" or "Ernest" if you scream those names at me at the mall). I was raised on free school lunches and "Reagan Cheese Giveaways." I am a product of musical discovery because of the school programs that allow children to find their true potential for greatness. I did in fact grow up poor, and I still remember the brutality of going hungry and being scared when everyone around me seemed destined for failure and pain. But those programs helped keep me alive, and still other programs like them helped give me confidence to hold my head up in the face of adversity and destitute despair. If it weren't for those programs, I'd have had no food in my belly, no road map to my future career, no shoes on my feet, no clothes on my back, no way of educating myself, and no real home to live in. Yes, there were issues in the houses I grew up in—and there were several, I'm telling you; however, there were people outside this circle of chaos who showed me the value in a hard day's work and the pride that could come from putting the hours in and coming out the other side stronger and more independent. I learned these lessons the hard-fought way and yet never abandoned my belief systems, even when I was homeless myself or when I was living and sleeping in a closet, or out of a bathtub, or in the back window of a car because the two toddlers were sharing the backseat itself. Oh yes, I know and remember every taste of every shade of shit I was forced to consume because at the time there was just no getting around it. But I never forgot who I was or what I wanted to be, aside from everything else: a good man who helped people who couldn't help themselves. Sometimes that's all you need as a subtle reminder or bookmark to the soul. Honestly, is that too much to ask?

I get it: shit is tough all over. No one wants to feel like they pay more than anyone else does. Well, if that's the case, why do you conservative supporters keep voting for politicians who raise taxes on you, the working class or lower class, only to lower taxes for those cocksuckers in the upper 1 percent who can actually afford to pay more? Don't believe me? Go back and look at their goddamn voting records. From Reaganomics to the new spending bill that the GOP is trying to push through Congress, they're gutting your ability to make a living, and doing it based on "alternative facts," like "a higher minimum wage hurts the poor"—what kind of bass-ackward fucking thinking is that shit? Guess what, morons: if you'd sort out the economy, the inflation rate would go down. If the inflation rate were down, YOU WOULDN'T NEED A HIGHER MINIMUM WAGE. By taking away all these regulations on big business and federal lobbying, you're driving that shit through the roof, putting more pressure on middle America. But you GOP-stopping sons-of-bitches only care about gilding your own pockets and those of the other cunts who help you stay in power. Just when the home run should go to the opposition—the party that feels and cares and speaks in terms that make hero speeches look like a drive-thru order—they not only go silent but slink away from the fight by and large. They do this under the auspices of keeping their integrity. I say they're too fucking scared to dig down in the fucking mud and find the shit that's buried beneath—and that's more than likely because they all have shit down underneath the surface. Below the topsoil they're all a bunch of bloodthirsty bottom-feeders, burying skeletons from their closets slower than they can keep killing in the name of morality. The cycle only breaks when the righteous man stands against the tides of tyranny. But no one is taking on those waves anymore, if they ever did to begin with.

Sometimes I wonder if the general public really gives a shit. It's got to be like *American Idol*—everyone voting for the one they like the most but never picking the one with the best abilities.

In the Age of Twits and Faces and Grams, the cheekbones are king and the "Eyes" have it. I can't even remember the last time we may or may not have voted for *anyone* from *any party* based on skill or know-how. It's always the motherfuckers who might look best on paper or at least are slinging the message at a rate that doesn't make the populace feel like knuckle-dragging cucks—except they really are. The joke is on all of us. This shit isn't about what they say they can do for us; if it were about that, we wouldn't still be slinging the same arrows and insults at each other—we might actually have changed things. But no one runs on real change. The only change that either side really wants to talk about is reversing all the "horrible choices" that the outgoing party has made in their policies. The Republican *may* be the worst at it—I saw on C-SPAN some fucking idiot member of the House saying that men shouldn't have to pay for prenatal care when it comes to insurance because "it doesn't have anything to do with men." HOW THE FUCK DOES THE GOP KEEP WINNING ALL THESE FUCKING SEATS WITH MORONIC VITRIOL LIKE THAT? That guy's lucky he hasn't been nutted so hard that when he shits himself, he can't feel it. So once again, how does the Democratic Party keep losing when they're up against such a pile of Man's Disease?

I've always been very vocal about my support for various individual freedoms and points of expression. I am an avid fighter against racism, bigotry, prejudice, bullying, sexual oppression, repression based on religious beliefs, and a host of other offenses that keep humanity trying to eat itself. I am pro-choice across the board. I am a firm believer in science, tech, truth, facts, right, wrong, justice, and the American way. I am a supporter of women's rights, civil rights, equal rights, and LGBT-plus rights . . . while *also* supporting law enforcement, military, our Second

Amendment rights, the right to steady work and equal hiring as well as equal pay. I believe in innocent until proven guilty just as much as I believe in capital punishment if the evidence is there and the guilt is clear and undeniable. I am a man of the center who isn't afraid to go to extremes on either side of the fence or aisle because that's what this country is. This country is men and women, many colors, many creeds, many sexual preferences and identities while *also* being full of the intelligent and the idiotic, the Right and Left, the snobby and civilized alike. It's no secret, so I'm still blown away when people act surprised when they find out that most Americans may be all over the map, but they're usually right near the center. There are zealots and fanatics on both sides, of course. But then again, who do you think drives people to the center? Hmm? It's certainly not our leaders. They're too busy leaning on the fence they're sitting on to worry about anything else, and if they're not doing that, they're just trying to accomplish all the ideas and policies that their *backers,* their *boosters,* their *lobbyists* have manipulated and paid them to get to the front of the political chow line. Make no mistake: we push ourselves to the middle where we feel the most comfortable. So why don't more of us vote that way? Why do the Republicans have a better track record of appealing to smart people *and* rubes (no offense, none taken) than the party who tries to do more for them than anyone else does? I think it's because the Democrats are not nearly as smart as they think they are.

Remember what I said about follow-through? This is another example of that same issue, the performance in the bedroom, so to speak. The liberals and the progressives and the Democrats and the Left all love to plan and plot and talk and plan some more, but when the work needs to be done, it's like they couldn't possibly be bothered to get down and dirty when it really matters. This is why the elites have so little practical understanding half the time: they're so used to hiring someone else to do the living for them. They muster up enough stamina to rail against the trials and tribulations that come from a party that only really wants to fund the military or their golf vacations, but when we need them to barrel down and get ready to rumble, they all conveniently "missed their bus." When it all comes down, the American people respect those who at least *act* like they're ready to get to work. I can't say that about three-fourths of the people currently affiliated with the Democratic Party, and even if I'm mistaken, that doesn't mean other people haven't come to the same assumption. Sometimes you've got to get those knees dirty just so you fit in with everybody else who's down digging in the fucking mud. There's no shame in it, and there's certainly nothing to really complain about when you start to think about it. You can't maintain a political party if you're too busy making everyone feel like they're not welcome. Identity goes both ways, and just assuming that anyone who looks or talks one way or another is going to be a Republican or, at any rate, a detriment, then you don't understand people. You don't understand society. You don't understand the feelings of a people who desperately need to be healed but don't know how to do it when their leaders are making us all feel like we're too different to have anything in common.

If Hillary could've remembered that, she might've had a chance. I still think she would've been a better president than the Cheeto, but sadly, she came off more like the White Queen than the Lady President. I pray that history rights the wrongs that so many muckraking bastards slung her way, but until that day, we can only hope that one or any Republican candidate has the grace in defeat that she has shown (unlike her supporters). If that simple example doesn't soften the glare of accusation against her, then these sawed-off motherless pricks can kiss my ass faster than you can reply with, "but her emails!" I hope the liberals stop drinking the purified bottled water around that time as well, seeing as the conservatives seem to get a sick joy out of pissing in it at the source. Let's just hope they didn't eat asparagus before they let it go—you'll smell it for miles. Then again, I just wish these "smart" Dems weren't that dumb.

Maybe it isn't too late to become a Libertarian . . .

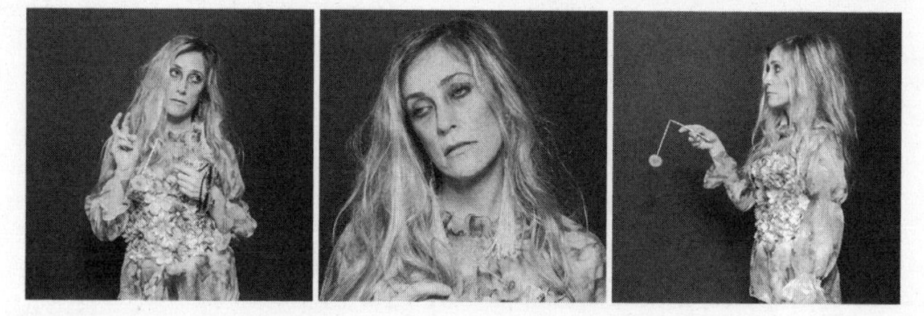

CHAPTER 6

THE GREATEST COUNTRY ON TURF

I WAS DRIVING AROUND IN THE SEPTIC CESSPOOL I LIKE to refer to as Los Angeles, California, one beautifully shitty day when a rich person's personalized license plate nearly pushed me to the brink of a *Death Proof* auto-violence rampage. Now that I've written that out, it makes me realize I've almost been driven (PUN!) to murdering behind the wheel quite a bit in California. I'm not sure why this is the case. It could be because I have unresolved anger issues that are in deep need of psychoanalysis. Another reason is that people in that Pacific coastal state have the urgency of a loose stool being pushed by a flaccid sphincter. Yeah, yeah, yeah, sue me for being a cock punch—those indy hippies need to stop saving shit and get the fuck out of my damn way. I don't care what kind of hair wax they use on their taint bristles, they don't need to walk slowly across streets or drive glacially while they talk about said sack wax.

Sorry, I'll get on with it.

Anywho, I was driving to Sphere Studio where Stone Sour was recording *Hydrograd* when a stoplight caught me before I could hammer the gas and get through it. So I was sitting there, listening to Ludacris, when my gaze gradually began to comprehend the Chevy Tahoe in front of me. Now, I have no issues with Tahoes—I have one myself. However, this one had a lot of trimmings that screamed "ball bag." There were bedazzled accoutrements *all over* the truck for no real reason. I could've understood if it were a girl's car (PROFILING!), but it also had chauvinistic stickers on it, like "No Fat Chicks" and "Ass, Gas, or Grass." I guess it would be chauvinistic of me to assume the sex of the driver either way, so I'll just say it sucked. Truly, surely, eternally sucked like a vortex of hardcore garbage abuse. Imagine the worst thing you could possibly think of on a genetic, emotional, and elemental level, then imagine it behind the wheel of this fucking truck.

I haven't even gotten to the fucking license plate yet.

It was while I was reading the painful stickers that I saw the vanity plate. I only use that term—vanity plate—when it comes to horrid attempts at humor. I took one look at it and knew that I either needed to get as far away from this car as I could or succumb to the urge to ram the shit out of it in order to get it off the road and save us all. Maybe I was being too harsh. You tell me—do you think this is funny?

"WASKLY 1"

Yep. That's what it said.

I've got to tell you: sometimes I question even the little bit of credit I give most people for their intelligence. But think about it this way: these vanity plates are pretty expensive. Most are between $80 and $100. Next, take into consideration the fact that most states have stringent laws *against* vanity plates (isn't that some shit? They'll offer them to you, but then they'll ticket you for having them). So you're spending a lot of money for something you may be ticketed for, and the *best* fucking idea you could *possibly* come up with in line while at the DMV was "WASKLY 1"? I mean, REALLY? You're *such* a huge Warner Brother Cartoons fan that you felt compelled to paraphrase a secondary character and have it pressed into steel? I know I may sound like an uber-maniac right now, but Judas Ahab and Don Quixote! WASKLY 1?

This could be the real epidemic in America: pure, unspoiled, and manic ignorance. I can't think of another country on the planet where the dichotomy between savvy and stupid has reached such huge proportions that Evel Knievel would have gladly jumped it in the 1970s. Some people treat real information like poisoned apples, while others hoard real information just to discredit people without it in a disdainful manner. I don't know. At this point maybe there's no saving any of us. There are so many things to worry about these days: morons who believe fake news stories, then attack people; morons who believe every conspiracy theory about the current administration; morons who are a part of the current administration; morons who *used to be* a part of the current administration (BYE, FLYNN) . . . and something just occurred to me: I'm worried about the cupcakes. What do we do if the cupcakes become self-aware and rise up against us, their creators? What do you *mean* we don't have a plan? I AM EXTREMELY WORRIED ABOUT THE CUPCAKES!

You get my point.

You know those strange personality tests you can take online? The ones where you answer a bunch of weird leading questions to find the answers to queries such as, "Which member of *Star Trek* are you?" or "Which house of Hogwarts would you be sorted into?" or even "Which cast member from *Supernatural* would you fall in love with?" You know the ones—they're never right, no matter how many times you take it to try to end up with Dean, but you always wind up with Castiel, and that's fine, don't get me wrong, but Cas always seems a little . . . never mind, you didn't read that, and I never wrote it. This was just an example! It was a joke! Who cares if *maybe* I know someone who *might* have been burned because of unrequited love! Right? No? You're not buying it, are you? Damnit . . . FINE! Abort! ABORT MISSION!

Anyway, you know the tests I mean. They give you a little commemorative meme to congratulate you on "being a member of . . . GRYFFINDOR House!" or "according to your answers, you are . . . SPOCK!" It's a tedious process for very little payoff, really. Still, it got me thinking about something interesting: What if there were a test like this, a sorting-by-personality test I mean, that would tell you what part of the country you should live in? Now, I know that seems a *little* like profiling and/or prejudice. But imagine that: taking the test, being assigned a "quadrant," and suddenly official-looking people were knocking on your door, ready to assist you in your "relocation." Insane, huh? Well, the truth is that a lot of people in America think that's actually a good idea. Doesn't exactly *smack* of "freedom of choice" or "open borders," now does it? Oh, and not to toss salt in the craw or anything, but the Nazis did that with the Jews, shuttling them into as many ghettos as possible before the unfortunate move toward the camps. When you're trying to uproot folks from their homes and their lives simply because you don't agree with their way of life, their beliefs, their marriage, or their rights in general, you are no longer living in a democracy. You are living in a fascist state, and I doubt that *anyone* who served this country to preserve freedom would agree that that's what he or she fought for.

I'm getting the feeling that the lynch mob is starting to muster, setting their sights on little ol' me and my big ol' neck. I could be wrong, but I can smell the torches lighting up, so let me clear some brush and move into some friendlier waters for a few minutes. We can just all chill out and relax for a second or two, catch our breath, reset, and hopefully find some ground around us that won't shake or quake with fear and resentment. This seems to be the crisis these days: whatever do we do when none of us can come up with a simple plan on how to *not* fucking fight all the time? Shit on shingles, we can't even have a casual chat about things like TV shows or cars anymore. I've seen grown-ass men cursing each other to early baldness and premature ejaculation because one hates *NCIS* and the other loves it, quoting all the Gibbs Rules while his opponent keeps from spitting in the other's face. That happened last month. I backed out of spitting distance before fleeing for drier climes. I remember thinking, *And today started out with* such *potential.*

Everybody needs to fight sometimes, but not over how awesome Abby is. That just goes without saying: Abby rules. But I have strong feelings about a lot of that dumbass shit in our country. We're going to pick a bunch of it apart very soon—like gun control and reproductive rights (I know I have the daddy parts, but I promise, I'm very pro-choice). Some of you are most likely going to ball up some fists and dog-ear this book a little too violently at these revelations, and that's fine too. It's my right to say what I think just as much as it's your right to disagree with what I have to say—even if you *are* wrong. Such is the fate of the American: one person's absolutes are another person's difference of opinion. I have several friends, on both sides of the aisle, I am constantly debating shit with. All it takes is a hard restart at the end of it all to get back on the Friend Train. We've gotten good at it because it means that much to us: the spirited quarrels and derring-do spiraling about our heads like a Cirque du Soleil show. Can you imagine how boring it would be to agree with *everything* that *everyone* said? Christ, I'd slice my own bollocks off just to have something to argue over.

You might be thinking, *Corey Taylor is a COMMIE! He hates our freedom! He hates our guns! He hates . . . hell, he hates ANYTHING AMERICAN!*

You'd be . . . well, you'd be a *little* right, but not really.

It's silly to claim that I hate anything American. This country is loaded with awesome shit, no matter its history or track record. Now, granted, as the living embodiment of nearly everyone's boogeyman/devil/oppressor (that, of course, being the white, heterosexual, meat-eating, atheist, American male), I feel like this might be a lesson in futility, trying to get most of you to see this place as anything other than the Orwellian ideal or a future state of Russia. You're absolutely right to regard me as automatically having a shit-load of strikes against me, rendering my arguments or endorsements a bit on the dingy side, to put it mildly. I get it—I really do. I read the paper (fuckin' A right, I still read the paper), I watch the news (fuckin' A right, I still have some trust in the MSM, aka the mainstream media), and I spend a lot of time on social media sites (fuckin' A right, I . . . actually I have no pithy retort for that proclamation—a man my age probably shouldn't be spending that much time on Twitter with those maniacs nor sending that many selfies out on Instagram; I can only apologize so much). So yeah, I like to think of myself as pretty informed. There is turmoil and anger rampant in the United States of America.

But if we all look pretty closely, we might see some really cool shit to be thankful for.

What about turducken?

Yes, you're reading that absolutely correctly: turducken. For those of you not familiar with what this is, let me explain it to you as best as I can, hopefully without a lot of snickering and giggling—or, worse yet, retching and vomit noises. For any vegans out there, you have my condolences, and you may want to skip ahead to a paragraph that feels fairly meatless. For any carnivores still committed to the definition of the aforementioned turducken, strap your asses to those planks and get ready to be either repelled or triggered into hunger pangs. Are you ready? Here we go: turducken (and, god help me, I hope I'm spelling that right) is, simply put, a chicken stuffed in a duck stuffed into a turkey. I can almost *see* you scratching at the gray lady upstairs. That's right, and yes, I will repeat myself: turducken is chicken stuffed in a duck stuffed in a turkey. It's kind of like an original American Jenga puzzle, flossing and flying through the layers and trying to get that one perfect bite with equal parts of the three birds in tow on your fork. Well, of *course* they take the fucking bones out—what kind of a crazy fucking question is that?

I bring it up because it is an example of pure American ingenuity. This dish owes its conception to the specialty meat shops of Louisiana, and although whom to credit with its invention is certainly up for discussion, the fingerprints of this beloved amalgam of meats is pure Americana. You can't escape the audacity of the enterprise: anyone could put one bird inside of another. But who in the sweetest of motherfucks would think to stuff one inside one, then stuff *those two combined* inside another? "Simply because you can" just doesn't begin to truly cover it. It takes a keen eye for the best way to super-size the fuck out of something already pretty fucking bitchin'. It's a culinary masterpiece that will never cry "fowl" (I'M NOT SORRY!), and although our British cousins have a reputable offshoot called *gooducken* (chicken stuffed in a duck stuffed in a *goose*), it genuinely doesn't come near the rotisserie beauty that is the definite article, turducken.

If you haven't tried it, I'll be honest, it's a bit greasy. Okay, it might be really greasy. Also, depending on where you get it from, it might have a semigamey taste to it. Nothing to worry about: that could be your taste buds getting used to so much poultry all at once. I will say that if you're going to get into your first bout with turducken, make sure you pick a light workweek. It *does* have a tendency to fight back, and you should look for the nearest exit if you understand the vernacular. I'm not saying it's not delicious; I *am* saying you might shit someone else's pants.

See? Off to a great start on this American Cavalcade of High-Velocity Awesome! What else can we talk about? Highways made out of shredded recycled tires? No, that couldn't be us—too thoughtful. I will say I am a fan of some of the more "on the edge" inventions in the last few years. The Bacon Bowl definitely comes to mind. I ranted about this on my tour for *You're Making Me Hate You*. Christ, you want to talk about defeating the purpose of eating a fucking salad in the first place, here comes a device that allows you to create salad bowls out of bacon. The Bacon Bowl is a contraption that does what it says. But how many other applications can something that fucking specific have, really? You going to try to make a bowl out of bologna with your Bacon Bowl? It won't work; it's a different viscosity. Maybe a crepe bowl, but you'd be better off working with one of those taco bowl makers if you're going to try that; that would seem about the right speed for that. If the creators of the Bacon Bowl want to fucking impress me, hit me up when they've patented and mass-produced the Bacon Piñata. *That* is something I would be fucking stoked about! Could you imagine a giant, fuck-off piñata made of motherfucking *bacon*?! Holy China shit! I'd shit twice, eat some more, shit again, and then die. I can't think of anything more impressive than the Bacon Piñata.

That is, unless you want to talk about the Bug-A-Salt.

Now, when I was a kid, I used to go out running the streets, empty lots, and fields, looking for places to hang out and play with my friends. Well, I say "play," but really I mean "smoke cigarettes and divvy up stolen goods while getting high and drunk." Yeah, I agree: they *were* simpler times. Anyway, there were some places where we *could* go, then there were some places that were straight up verboten. These were usually fields owned by someone else who kept an eye on them for fear of shit-stains like us coming around and either defacing an outbuilding or setting fire to some tall grass by accident. The reason I bring it up is because the threat was almost always the same: "The farmer who owns that lot, he walks around with a shotgun loaded with nothing but shells full of rock salt! It won't kill you, but it'll sting like crazy—it might even blind you!" Maybe it was just the people I hung out with, but we were convinced that everyone who guarded their property had nothing but rock salt to use as ammunition. In hindsight I have a sneaking suspicion that my friends and I were just really fucking stupid . . . or high . . . or both—yeah, that's a possibility too.

Now, thirty fucking years later, here comes this fucking invention called the "Bug-A-Salt." How do I sum this up? The Bug-A-Salt is a plastic Nerf-looking shotgun of sorts specially designed for loading with table salt so you can shoot flies and other insects with it. The commercials are fucking *legit* too: every time they shoot said insects, they're *always* sitting on some sort of foodstuff, like green Jell-O that wiggles madly when the spray hits it, or a nicely assembled fruit bowl, or a loaf of fucking bread. It is high-larious to say the absolute least. I very nearly ordered a couple dozen for my own house—not for the insects but to keep vigilant watch on any transgressions on my lawn by teenagers, especially if I didn't like the cut of their jib. Yes, I've effectively become the cranky crotchety cunt fending off intruders on his postage stamp of grass for fear they'll try to take it . . . or just mess up my grass, really. Plus, I don't want them wearing out a path on my shit.

Folks, I've done a lot of things in my life I'm very fucking proud of. I've written hit songs and popular books, been in movies and on television, and toured the world, and I've had a fucking blast doing it. But if I can be brutally truthful with you for this one moment, I'll tell you: there's a part of me that would seriously like to kick my own ass for not coming up with something as crazy and unique as a goddamn Bug-A-Salt. I'm the old lady in the Kohl commercial who lives the full life, only to be hit with a flour sack full of regret because she died before getting to take a bath in some nifty tub across the way. That also could mean I watch a little too much fucking television. Yes, because I don't sleep a lot. I don't sleep because I can't stop thinking. I can't stop thinking because I'm a manic nightmare of a human. I'm a manic nightmare of a human because I don't sleep . . . you get the picture.

I *still* want one of those things. Then again, so do a lot of dumb people.

Look, I've gone on record several times stating that I am not immune to this idiocy. I'm just as dipped in dipshit as the rest of you cretins. The difference? I make this shit look really good. Okay, maybe that's not completely true. In fact, I'm quite sure there are people—who I enjoy, mind you—who are very aware of my sporadic bouts with the mental vacuum. Take for instance the sad, lonely tale of the immortal dumbass question, "Bear or goat?" Yes, this is a true story. Yes, the memory alone is incredibly embarrassing for yours truly. Yes, the thought of retelling it to you makes me want to puke across my stress-induced cold sores.

Am I going to tell it anyway? Of course I am, because I've always been very clear that there is very little I will not do in the never-ending quest to keep you pricks entertained. So sit back, relax, nurse the three fingers of Scotch you dumped in your child's favorite superhero glass because all your fancy ones are dirty as fuck, and we'll begin.

Some of you may not have heard about this, but many moons ago my wife and I were invited to a taping of *Tosh.0*. We were super-excited because we rarely get to do stuff like that, so we went with some friends, got a tour of the offices where they write the show, saw the green-screen rooms where a lot of it is filmed, and eventually got to meet Daniel himself. We sat down to watch the taping of the show, which they do twice to allow for different jokes that pop up and for more genuine excitement. During the filming Daniel was looking over at me and asking me about Slipknot lyrics while also demonstrating the alternative interpretations he'd come up with for songs like "Eyeless" (there's no real way to spell them correctly, so I'll just put "ASHGREATTNEUNFRNYBRBBCviu"!) At the end of the first taping there was a segment where he tried to set the record for most people in a line being electrocuted at once with a power cell for an electric fence. He then explained that the box was set on "goat," but he hadn't found anyone to try it on the "bear" setting. Between takes he intimated that he should have it brought out and get a member of the audience to try it out. He then looked directly at me.

I knew then that I wasn't going to leave that night . . . without getting electrocuted.

And so the show rolled—once again with the tapings, the jokes, different jokes, different reactions, and so on. Cut to the electrocution bit. The box is now out on the sound stage on a chair with two long metal wires coming off it. The joke is said:

"Luckily this was set on goat—we couldn't find anyone to try it out set on bear," and immediately he looks in my direction. Daniel Tosh smiles and says, "You want to try it?" Of course I said "no"—as I was standing and making my way to the stage. He turned it on and moved out of the way for me to grab the wires (that was the worst part: I had to grab the wires and do it to *myself*). After a few botched attempts to get a hold of them and complete the circuit, I was finally successful. The shock was tremendous; I immediately dropped the wires and skipped around the stage, cursing the man and his new-fangled lightning machine. To his true credit, as soon as I did it and dropped the wires, he snatched them up and did it too so I wouldn't be the only one in dire pain. By the way, you can see *all* of this in the special features of Tosh's DVD *Completely Serious,* or on YouTube, as it's been posted up there in the subsequent years. The show was wrapped, we all laughed, and it was considered a great taping. If only I'd gone home after that, I wouldn't be telling this little revealing anecdote . . .

After the rest of the audience had left, we again went backstage to visit with some of the writers and with Daniel. I was still drinking at the time, so I helped myself to a couple of beers. We were all talking and having fun. I excused myself to go find the bathroom. When I came out, Daniel was standing there and asked me if I was feeling okay. I said for someone who'd just been shocked to shit and back, sure, I felt great. He told me he wanted to make sure because of the lawyers and whatnot. "I'm just glad the thing was set on goat," I said with a laugh. He chuckled at my memory of the joke—but I wasn't quoting the joke. You'd think that a man who grew up in Iowa would have a grasp on the workings of an electrical fence circuit. I'd love to blame the beer, but I can't for one reason: I asked him again, "Was that thing set on goat or bear? Anybody try that high a setting?" He kind of giggled and shook his head, wandering off. It wasn't until later when it suddenly hit me: THERE ARE NO ANIMAL SETTINGS ON THOSE BOXES. I'd basically made a legitimate fucking fool out of myself in front of one of the smartest, funniest cats on the planet. To this day I wonder if he has ever thought, *Dude, that singer for Slipknot* really *took that joke fucking literally.*

Eh. If it ever came down to it, I'd just blame the bolt of energy that had charged through me for my momentary lapse of reason. I'm sure I'd win in court, but in my head I'd still be the fuckhole who made an ass out of himself. I know it's not a specifically American thing to do, but it feels supremely intense when Americans wipe their ass with their gray matter. I have a theory about this: I think it's because that much freedom allows you to go off the deep end with what you choose to accept or reject as real useful information. We talked earlier about some of the conspiracies running rampant out there. From collusion with Russia to the basement of Comet Pizza, it's a fucking madhouse. People pick or disregard based on their own passions, *not* based on reporting or facts. That's because, much like the regulatory systems on our various branches of government, there are no true checks and balances kept in place. The "news story" has been outdone by the "editorial." It's like these fucking mooks who insist that creationism should still be taught right next to evolution in school because, they claim, there are "too many holes in the theory and people deserve a choice." ON WHAT FUCKING PLANET ARE THERE HOLES IN THE THEORY OF EVOLUTION? They are so fucking terrified by the comfort of facts that they will fight common sense tooth and nail until they die. The same thing goes for these idiots who perpetuate "alternative facts" and fucking "fake news." The levels of petulance and privilege in people who are perfectly all right with advancing these ideas are so far off the charts that I can't fucking believe they haven't been rounded up, stuffed into mental facilities for observation, and, finally, singled out for shock therapy. The people who teach creationism over evolution based on religion are most likely the same people who teach physics based on cartoons: *morons*.

That reminds me: remember Howard Dean? Yeah, I've talked about him before. Howard Dean's path to the presidency was essentially destroyed with a "Byah!" That was it; that was all it took to ruin a man's climb to the top. One big "Byah!" and it was over. I'm sure there was more to it than that—there always is. I'm still trying to wrap my head around the fact that Al Gore never ran again. Maybe there's something massive in *his* closet too. Now you can be a viable candidate while still grabbing them by the pussy, like a fucking bowling ball for Christ's sake. One man's "Byah!" is another man's boom stick, I guess. Plus, who'd have thought we'd be able to Google nudes of the First Lady? No, I do *not* mean Ivanka Trump, and I am just as fucking grossed out as everyone else who refers to Trump's daughter as the First Lady. Then again, if you saw some of the footage of the way he acts and what he says about her, I suppose I'd be confused if I were the American public as well. Does that put it all together for you now? More people think Trump's daughter is his wife than people who think he was elected legitimately. Nah, don't Google that: I just made that stat up and I ain't even sorry for it. The Cheeto can kiss my ass.

Sorry. Let's get back to more things that make America great. (Not "again." This country has always been great; white people just wish it were "whiter again.")

All right, fine: the country's pulled some shit on quite a few people. Hundreds of years of persecution and slavery is hard to sweep under the rug. Incarceration and forced interment has a way of taking the shine off the American Apple. We—as a nation, mind you—have mistreated our citizens of color and our creed so bad over the years that not even "reparations" have settled the score. Most white folks think the only colors in our country that count are red, white, and blue: white people with red necks and blue collars. Now, I got nothing against blue collars. Without them, we have no foundation. We'd have no roads, no buildings, no utilities, no anything. However, there are people other than whites who are part of the working class. Someday I'd like to do a study on why most Caucasians aren't very inclusive. Until then I'll keep gently reminding the gentiles that they are in fact *not* the only fucking people in this country and on this planet. Get your fucking shit together, honkies, and if you don't like it, you can fucking suck it, Trebek.

Anyway, enough about that shit. Let's talk about man buns.

I know what you're thinking, and yes, I am going to shit on a gigantic part of our culture right now. It's not because it's specifically American—the Chinese and Japanese were using versions of the man bun centuries ago. Hell, even David Beckham was wearing one a few years before it was officially a thing. But leave it to Americans to make it suck. What was once a sign of the warrior class and athleticism became the common hairdo of the pretentious cunts known as the hipsters, by all virtue making it neither hip nor manly. I regret my handful of forays into wearing a pseudo bun because of how shitty everyone around me looked while stuck in them. They all looked like hippie versions of Marvin the Martian auditioning for a role in a shitty western. Bollocks. Then again, I guess you'd *have* to look that way playing that excuse for "rock" they were going for. That was a great idea: "Hey! As a reaction to all the auto-tuning, beat detecting, pitch correcting, overproducing, super-compressing, and all the other shit that has made modern music suck a bag of soggy soft dicks, we'll play everything for real, except we'll only use shit like accordions and banjos while white boys with no talent punch away on Casio samplers! We'll call it rock!"

That shit doesn't rock. As interesting as that shit sounds, it's *not* rock. You can call it aggressive folk or banjo funk, but not rock. Come on, what the hell? Seriously? Fine, whatever, but let me tell you something: when you go to a hipster concert, you leave and update your status while you wait for a lavender latte and a Lyft. When you go to a rock concert, you're either too fucking tired to do anything but go home or you're so drunk that you wake up somewhere, find a way home, and tell your friends all about it. That's the difference between a real rock concert and that shit that ended up in the "rock" category. Everyone can hate me all they want—this is the face of a man who hasn't had a fuck to give since 1991. I don't care about your senseless sensibilities or your fucking vaginal tendencies. You all need to pull your balls and ovaries out of your pockets, roll them around in some mud for a second, and get back in the fucking game because hell is following right behind me, and it don't give a damn about safe places or feelings or whatever. I'll paraphrase a great song title: NUT UP OR SHUT UP.

That's the thing: you think we're friends. We're not friends. You *think* you know me, but you don't, and I don't know you from Adam and the Ants. I can almost guarantee you that there are a million things I hate about you, from the way your face is glued to that shitty phone in your hand to the look of annoyance that darkens that same face when someone *deigns* to step on your privilege sensors by doing something completely uncalled for, like asking if they can borrow an unused chair at your table. I have *watched* people roll their eyes and turn away like cock-bites because they couldn't be bothered to deal with the human race for ten fucking seconds. So much of this country is built on ego, elitism, petulance, and anger that it makes my fists ball up when I don't realize it. You know what bugs me the most about this country? The fact that so many people were so bummed out on Obama that they thought the Cheeto was a viable option. *That's* fucking America right there—so much fucking freedom that they'd put themselves in harm's way a million times over just to prove they were right all along.

Once again, that's the problem we're experiencing right now. No one feels like they're being heard, no matter what's being said. That's why the Cheeto has gotten as far he has: by taking advantage of the cultural rift where the silence is reflected back on itself and communication disappears. Twenty years ago Trump would've been laughed out of the lobby of his own hotels for trying to declare his candidacy. Now? He's the fucking Republican president, a Republican president who mocks (and you can look it up—oh, and fuck you if you defend it, you chicken shits) people with disabilities, women, other races, *anyone* who doesn't agree with him, reporters—basically everybody. There's a reason for that: he's a bullying cunt. I know it feels like the Left are doing most of the bullying lately, but that's because an ass hat who is completely unqualified for the highest office in our country is slowly but surely wiping his ass with the integrity of the post. Oh, he's also a hypocritical coward as well. Notice his rallies get farther and farther south.

He *talks* a great fucking game, and yet *how many* engagements has he canceled because he couldn't handle the protests? Hmm? At least two? Yeah, you're pretty tough, Trump. It's the same reason he doesn't answer questions. Maybe if he talked and really listened more while accusing less, people wouldn't be taking over his rallies to protest him. Maybe his Republican senators and members of the House of Representatives wouldn't be hounded at town hall meetings and political roundtables. Maybe his team would have a half-assed plan instead of a bunch of faulty doctrine triggered by those fucking hate groups he's trying so hard to impress. There's that old saying that "sometimes all you need is hope." His supporters are those people, for whatever reason. They hang on his words like rope swings in summer. They believe him like a reference book. They put their faith in him because what else do they have? They are running on outdated software that only made sense with a few old servers. When the time came for the upgrades, no one could handle the downloads—it wasn't compatible with their systems anymore. So now they've created a savior out of a demagogue in expensive, ill-fitting suits and a horrid comb-over. They think he's doing more than he actually is, while he's putting a hurt on the money drain—way more than the nice black gentleman who preceded him. What do you think is going to happen when the bottom falls out of their custom-made fantasy?

I once wrote that the American Dream—not Dusty Rhodes but the ethereal equivalent—is the mindset that built the foundation for our country and created a myth for the rest of the world. I described it as an opportunity, nothing more, and people have since bastardized it to mean "get rich quick" or "use the system to fuck others over for your own gains." That's not what the American Dream was meant to be. It was intended to be the chance to pick up the pieces of your life and rebuild it in a place where safety is granted under the ceiling of freedom and sanity. So generations of the poor, the tired, and the huddled masses came to our shores to find sanctuary and peace while raising a family of next-gen Americans. This was another part of the blue-collar population, the ones who rolled up sleeves and got down in the dirt to make sure the legs were sturdy and the buildings were "purdy." Those of the paler complexions have chosen to be slightly myopic when it comes to who they let in the blue-collar class reunion, but it would be a fucking travesty of justice to omit those from foreign lands who came, earned their citizenship, and stayed to help make this country stronger.

Now an American president (not *my* president, but *the* president) is trying his damnedest to block refugees and immigrants from coming to this country, and he's doing so under the guise of "keeping us safer" (read: "keeping us whiter"), thereby feeding the unfounded fears of his constituents (read: "peasants"). Never mind that the places he's trying to put the ban on have never been a terrorist threat to us. Never mind the fact that more Americans are in danger of being killed by white extremists (read: *terrorists*) than Muslims from the countries Trump has singled out. No, let's keep people paranoid and suspicious of those who aren't the same color as them while domestic terrorists are released because according to the new laws, white people can't be tried as terrorists. Yes, you read that right. Yes, that's a true statement. The gentleman who was gearing up to bomb Target stores will not have terrorist charges brought against him because the laws have been rewritten to skew in favor of Caucasians and against Muslims. It seems like every fucking day something happens or is reported or comes out in a leak that drives me to want to set my fucking face on fire and run around head-butting people while I squirt them with gasoline.

I have every confidence that this book is going to "lose me some fans." I have no illusions about it. Hopefully most people struggle through to the other chapters that are a little more balanced. Right now you're probably reading this and saying, "Judas fucking Priest, he's a cryin' snowflake cuck." Fair enough. But if you take anything from this book, it should be this: I still believe in the American Dream, which is now about chasing the ideal of what we told the world we were *supposed* to be. Now it's about putting our oil money where our gold-toothed mouths are. It's about backing up freedom of speech and healthy debate. There are a lot of people in this country who don't understand that the blanket works both ways. So I take this chance to remind you all of the wonders of the First Amendment and all the glories intimated on that glorious document. It's taken a while for some of those freedoms to catch up with everyone here, and they are certainly taking a few hits here and there right now, under siege from the bourgeoisies who say they speak for the working class while gutting all the ways working-class folks can get ahead. Sure, we've got issues. But we also have the tools to deal with those . . . well, tools.

America promises a lot. It shines in the night like one of those searchlights you see in World War II films or like the ones you always see near the malls or downtown areas, doing the circular programmed motions in the dark. It has been a beacon for anyone willing to risk for gain. We have totally shit on some people's aspirations over the years, but I maintain that we're still out there trying to do the good work. We'll talk more about how I think we should stick a little closer to our own backyards for a while and how domesticity might actually help us even out our shitty little empires, but for now let's just focus on that message: "The land of the free and the home of the brave." This is not just a sweet lyric to our national anthem; it is a credo I think we all, as a whole, put a lot of stock and pride in. I know I do. I've always believed that more people fight harder when they're defending a country *worth* fighting for than when they're fighting for one that sucks. There's a different energy that manifests itself in the breasts and bellies of our populace, our militia, and our military. We stand for something that may or may not be true anymore, but as long as the mindset is still there, the belief can make the vision become visceral. It can make the steel in the eyes harder than the steel in those bayonets and bullets. We have never tolerated tyrants and despots before, and I don't think we're going to start anytime soon, you feel me?

This is why I'm not very concerned about the Cheeto. If he doesn't get his shit together, the country will rise and take him down in one giant revolution. Thomas Jefferson said there should be a revolution every twenty years to keep the government honest. Maybe that's what it'll finally take to put us back on the map. Until then I'll just keep putting the quotation marks around our tried and true phrase "the greatest country in the world" while I wait for the facts to catch up to our fiction.

CHAPTER 7

YOU DON'T SPEAK ENGLISH

PEOPLE TALK TO ME—SPEAK AT ME, ACTUALLY—ALL THE time about adversity. Especially my fellow countrymen; god, they *love* to babble on about rising above the odds or to the challenge and not letting the weird shit bring you down. I believe this is why Americans love shows like *Survivor* or *The Amazing Race*: they like to think they'd excel if the roles were reversed and the spectators were there instead, rallying all of their rationale and resources to overcome even a sort of manufactured adversity because "Americans will always win. Americans are winners, and whatever obstacle we come up against, we'll inevitably come out the victor. It's what we do—we win." From Reagan to the newest round of shit like that from Trump, we patriots from the fifty states are pretty stubborn in our global championship assessment. To them, there's nothing that can't be fixed, beaten, figured out, or made to work with the help of a whole bunch of people chanting "USA! USA! USA! USA!" So, fundamentally speaking, you'd *think* that we 'Muricans would be all gung ho to go out into the world in search of adventure and excitement in exotic locales, among different cultures, and slipping in and out of cool dialects and such.

On that note I'm about to tell you a really sad and pathetic story.

I know, that's sort of out of character for a CMFT book, but sometimes I feel the need to add hints of melancholy here and there. Plus, this book has tended to skew very dark and angry—not that fun kind of angry like my other literary tirades, but the "god damnit, I really hate having to point out this dipshit nonsense" type of angry. Honestly, I can't believe you guys have soldiered *this* far through this bastard. But that's why you come to me: for the dollar bills, reality checks, and incredible cheek bones—TRUTHFULNESS! I meant to say *truthfulness.* Anyway, before I get too far up my own ass, let me first explain *why* I'm going to tell you this story: because if you haven't noticed from my book or from the rest of the crap around us all, we the people of the United States of America are so full of fucking shit about ourselves that brown should be the fourth color on our flag. I'll fill you in more on what I mean, but you'll first need an example, and oh boy fuckin' howdy, do I have one for you. It involves an FOB, a quick trip to Japan, copious amounts of booze, a strip club run by the Jamaican mob, and a lost/stolen passport. Yep, strap on your big-kid helmets because it's about to get fucking ignorant.

First off, let's answer the question sitting in your mouths like the cinnamon challenge: What the fuck is an "FOB"? Well, any traveling musician will tell you that FOB stands for "friend of band." An FOB isn't usually an issue. Most times a FOB can mean exactly that or it can be longtime fans that became close to the band over the years and are now considered FOBs. Those examples are fine; they're actually pretty awesome because I've grown extremely close to some of my FOBs. However, there's another section of FOB: the ones who claim to be techs, or roadies, for lack of a better term, but have no real idea of what goes into being on the road or how a person is supposed to function/conduct him or herself. Fortunately, for the benefit of your entertainment, this story concerns the latter example. Unfortunately, I had to live through it to be able to share it with you all. For *his* benefit, I'll change his name to Dick. I'll also downplay his involvement with the band for anonymity's sake because I don't want it to blow back on my people. But trust me: Dick doesn't deserve your sympathy. Dick is a fucking tool-bag of the lowest caliber and should have never been hired in the first place, let alone allowed to get on the plane with us.

But I digress . . .

Let me set the scene a little better. The band was picking up a couple of shows in Japan before embarking on a North American tour, and because of that we didn't have our core crew, the crew we would be using for the duration of the tour itself. Figuring we could get by with a few fill-ins because these were just a couple of shows, we brought on a few newbies as well as Dick, who had never left the country before yet talked a great game about "knowing everything there is to know about guitars, and I'll be fine on the road, don't you worry—you'll have to keep up with *me*!" We as a band collectively shrugged and made our way to Japan. If you've never been there, it is truly a gorgeous country, full of robust urban landscapes blended with natural majesty and tranquility. The people are quiet but friendly, and the pace depends on where you are: in the cities like Tokyo and Osaka it is frenetic and crisp, while outside, in places like Fukuoku, it is definitely more laid back. But it has a little bit of something for everyone. For me, I've been blessed to have a major following there, so I was really excited for the shows because I knew we were going to have an amazing time. We landed, were met by fans and management at the airport, and were taken to the hotel. We checked in, dropped off our passports at the front desk, as is custom there, and we all tried to dodge the jet lag as best we could by going to sleep. Unbeknownst to me, however, when we all split up, a certain FOB decided he was going to go exploring.

Cut to the next morning at lobby call . . .

We all made our way down to the bus that would be taking us over to the gig. Some of us had indeed been able to sleep, while others had suffered at the hands of jet lag's evil insomnia and were now trying to fight their way through the pain by just staying awake the whole time. The band and crew mingled and talked shit, and when the bus arrived we all boarded and sat waiting for our tour manager, who hadn't made it yet. There was no sign of Dick. None of us were worried; we had a few hours until we played, so we consigned ourselves to sitting and waiting. Eventually our tour manager *did* join us on the bus. He was late, which was odd for him—usually he was the first one down to the lobby and the last one to get on the train, plane, or whatever. He seemed to be in a fairly terrible mood too, another sign that something was a bit off that day. Still missing, fairly conspicuously, was Dick. Questions were asked between us, only to be met with similar inquisitive looks. Our tour manager was alerted to his absence, and I swear to god this happened: our tour manager stiffened, his face went completely red, and he stormed off the bus back into the hotel.

Thirty minutes later in stomps our tour manager (TM), followed closely by a *fucked-up* Dick, severely hungover, reeking of flop sweat and stale beer. He collapsed into one of the seats on the bus and did not come back up. We were stunned at first, but with one look at the back of our TM's neck, which was getting redder and redder from anger, we knew we shouldn't ask too many questions. We rode in silence for an hour and a half, arriving at the venue with *just* enough time to set up our shit, play our show, and get *back* on the bus to return to the hotel. All the while we were all wondering just what in the ever-livin' fuck had happened to piss off our TM and leave Dick smelling like a Baptist preacher's dirty little secret. Over the course of the next couple of days we pieced together the events that led to Dick's shitty state and, subsequently, his early dismissal. You're going to *love* this shit . . .

After we'd all checked in and split, Dick decided he wanted to go out. He wanted to have some adventure. Fair enough—it's only natural, really. I can remember feeling the same way when I first came to Japan myself. This, however, is where the similarities end, because Dick broke every fucking unwritten rule in the tour handbook. Yes, there's an unwritten tour handbook. How the fuck should I know what it looks like—I'm sure it's probably leather bound and awesome looking, but it's hard to tell because it's unwritten. Of *course* I believe it's real—my friend told me about it. Which friend? You don't know him—he's from Canada. I met him at Niagara Falls. Yes, of *course* he's really real too! What the fuck is going on with this interrogation!? I'm uncomfortable with this line of questioning! You're just going to have to trust me! I have a friend from Canada, he *promised* he was real, and there's an unwritten handbook for the rules on touring! Now leave me alone before I tell my grandma you're being mean! God, you guys are assholes . . .

Here's what Dick did to set the stage for his spectacular disaster.

One, he left the hotel alone. Now let's pretend that you the reader are someone who's *never* been abroad your whole life. You arrive at night at your destination. Would *you* go out into a city like Tokyo by yourself, knowing absolutely *no Japanese?* Yeah, it's not a great fucking plan. Sailors descending into cannibalism make better decisions than that. But even this would have been sort of okay if not for number two on the list: he didn't tell *anyone* he was leaving. That's right: this fucking dipshit split the scene and didn't give anyone a head's up, in a sprawling metropolis of *many* millions, not knowing anything about anything. He just decided to go, and he went. I wouldn't be as irate with him to this day if he was, like, a kid or something. This man is *older than I am*. How the fuck do you get to be middle-aged and have no fucking clue about what you're doing? It's baffling, to say the least. Then again, once you hear the rest of the story, maybe it'll make more sense. So on his own and without telling anyone, Dick waded into the darkness of the Tokyo nightlife.

His next mistake was falling for one of the tourist honey traps. After hitting a few bars (and paying with his debit card instead of exchanging dollars for yen . . . insert rolling-eyes emoji face) Dick found himself wandering—*now drunk*—until a business barker hailed him, calling him over to invite him inside his establishment. Yeah, it was a strip club, but it was more than a strip club; it was an escort service ostensibly for higher-class clientele, run by Jamaican gangsters who'd emigrated there to work with local hoods. In other words, it was a place Dick was woefully not prepared to be caught dead or alive in. But supposedly, with a grin and a sweaty, thinning hairline, Dick bounced in, slapped his debit card down, and began drinking *fast*, bothering all the girls and pissing off the wrong motherfuckers in the process. You can almost *sense* where this is going, but I'll get you there anyway. It's pretty much exactly what you'd think, except way funnier and scarier.

After a couple of hours the nice gentlemen of the Jamaican mob came to the unanimous conclusion that they'd had about as much of Dick's company as they'd like to admit. So they told him he needed to pay his tab and leave. Dick, blind drunk and belligerent, surveyed the wall of beef stacked against him and calmed down a bit. He handed over his debit card as payment. Now, Dick is from the Midwest, with an account plan that isn't exactly suited to "exotic purchases," especially charges originating from an escort service in Tokyo, Japan. So, to NO ONE'S SURPRISE BUT ASSHOLE DICK HIMSELF, the card was rejected. This was largely because (a) he hadn't let the bank know he was going overseas, making sure they'd be alert for international charges, and (b) he hadn't researched the exchange rate enough to realize he was *way* over his fucking limit. Indeed, this moron was running around the Shibuya district like a fucking maniac, putting a major run on his card that wasn't going to balance at the end of the night. The greatest part of this story is that THIS ISN'T EVEN CLOSE TO HOW BAD IT'S ABOUT TO GET!

So the Jamaican mob goes to his table and demands he handle the rest of the money. Dick, still wasted but slowly becoming more and more paranoid, makes up his mind that they are not only trying to steal his debit card but that they've also stolen his passport (the passport, you may recall, that he'd left at the hotel). So in a moment of sheer manic panic, Dick accused them all of stealing his shit. You'll understand why his "hosts" didn't exactly like that. So they try to grab Dick, but dipshit managed to get away from them. He ran from the club, with a bunch of crazy Jamaicans right on his ass. Dick, covered in sweat, booze, and piss, found a local police station, burst in like Kevin McCarthy from *Invasion of the Body Snatchers,* and started screaming that the owners of the club were trying to kill and rob him. The police escort him back to the club, where the club members lay everything out for the officers, from his drunkenness to his inability to pay his bill. When Dick accuses them of stealing his things, they tell the officers he never had his passport and that they were holding his debit card until someone paid his *very* outstanding bill. The police looked around, asked some questions, and took Dick back to the station for his own safety and because until he could pay his bill, he was effectively under arrest.

The dude hadn't been in Japan more than five hours.

Right here is when our TM got the call—at 4 A.M. The police told him the predicament, to which our TM screamed a bit, had them put Dick on the phone so he could scream at *him* a bit, relented, and finally got dressed to come bail Dick's shitty stupid ass out. Our TM also had to pay the outstanding bill because, come to find out, it was even more than originally suspected, to the point where Dick was essentially working these shows for free because he was in so much debt to us. When Dick kept accusing the club of also stealing his passport, our TM angrily reminded him that he'd left his passport with the front desk, just like everyone else in the tour party. Dick was made to apologize, he got his debit card back, and our TM got him back to the hotel around 6 A.M.—about four hours before lobby call. Dick was summarily dismissed soon afterward—much to the relief and cheering of the whole band and crew. The guy was a shit-show from the very start, and as it turned out, he was just as big a fucking nightmare domestically as internationally. I could tell you a whole story about how this same Dick nearly ruined a meet-and-greet with a prominent guitar player all because he burst into his dressing room and began drinking all his beer, getting so drunk that his fucking ride left him in an alley passed out. But that's not what this chapter is about.

We spoke about that touring handbook earlier, and I'd be remiss if I didn't tell you there's another unwritten rule regarding being that far away from home, especially when you're a reasonable Yank traveling abroad: when people hear your accent, tell them you're Canadian, because Americans are some of the shittiest tourists/travelers on the face of whatever country they happen to be in at the time. That little Japanese trip is really just the tip of the iceberg; in fact, this more like the nose of the Titanic, because what did that iceberg do to anyone before that night? It was just minding its own business when out of nowhere, a giant cruise ship not paying attention to either Jack, Fuckin', or Shit came about and rammed the shit out of it. That's about as good a parable I can come up with for the way most asshole Americans act when they go on "holiday" anywhere other than their own backyard. I say *most* out of fairness, and I will stipulate that every country on the planet has its share of cock-knocking travel sets, but the brash American tourist has a special sort of entitled pettiness that is unrivaled even by the French, who are about as spiky as they get sometimes. I have nothing against the French, but I have experienced some severe treatment by French people and can truly say that it *has* to be because of other Americans' behavior while running amok on the Continent or anywhere else. Most Yanks tend to treat a vacation as a toilet, and whatever country they happen to be visiting sadly becomes the fanny ribbon they wipe their shitty assholes with.

I know a lot of Americans aren't going to like what I'm saying, but it's true. Sorry. I'm willing to bet you bullets to buttons that I'm out of the country more than most of you, and unfortunately, I see it all the damn time—American tourists walking around like they own the fucking place, talking loud, talking shit, complaining about EVERY GOD DAMN THING YOU COULD POSSIBLY

IMAGINE, and doing so directly into the faces of the kind locals just trying to get through their day. There is a special sort of indignant arrogance that emanates from us that I can only compare to the fallout we're still detecting in places like Chernobyl and Three-Mile Island, largely with the same devastating effects. We are the radioactive pricks of Planet Earth; I honestly can't believe that places abroad don't have detectors designed to go off anytime an American enters their establishments. Then again, they don't really need them, do they? There's an undeniable sound that gives fair warning way before it gets too tense in the stores, shops, restaurants, museums, and so on. That's right, you guessed it: the sound would be coming from our big, dumb, petulant, sewer-smelling American mouths, and half the time the shit we're saying is worse than the smell that's on our collective breaths.

"You don't speak English!?"

If I had a nickel for every time I've heard that at the table next to me in a restaurant abroad, I wouldn't need to be writing this book—I'd have retired to my island by now. But you need to understand something first: it's not the question itself. I've asked that question myself when the language barrier is a little too out of reach, but I've also followed that up with a smattering of my own crappy attempts at speaking the native tongue, whatever that language happens to be. No, no, this isn't about the question itself but about the vile disdain behind it when it comes from someone who cannot *possibly* fathom that someone who doesn't live in the good ol' US of fuckin' A can't speak or understand English. Never mind that most of the world tends to be fluent in at least two languages (except our country because we don't care). Never mind that most places have appropriate menus or people on staff who *do* speak English so that everyone gets what they want. Oh no, this is about the overwhelming entitlement that screams from almost every dildo who hails from in between Mexico and Canada on our North American continent. To these people, it's a personal affront to some sort of mythic history they've created in their heads having to do with whatever the fuck they think the world *owes* America for services rendered. To them it's amazing that anyone would have the audacity *not* to be fully functional in shitty English just in case the gilded cunts known as the Yanks come wandering for "whatever they call those things in Dubuque—you know, that place that always stinks of spices . . . a curry! Yeah, let's all get curries! It'll be fun!" To an American the rest of the world is basically just an extension of the United States. "Hell, we have military bases everywhere—we must own *most* of these places!" It's kind of eerie just how misinformed and ignorant most Americans are. I'd say it's surprising, but they elected the Cheeto, so the dead cat's out of the bag on that one.

I'm going to assume it has something to do with what we believe we contributed to the world wars, both I and II, as well as what people think has happened over the last thirty years as far as our foreign policy goes. Like I said before, I think a lot of Americans labor under the impression that the world *owes* us something—not that the world should be appreciative but that the entire planet *owes* us something because of our involvement in foreign affairs and conflicts. I'd wager a guess that they believe all the war movies: everyone's getting their asses *whipped* by the big, bad bone daddies of the Axis or the Kaiser and his assholes, things look bleak for the world—UNTIL! Here comes Ameri-fucking-ca, ready to do some damage on fascists and foes alike, just in time to save the day. When all appeared on the verge of collapse, the Red, White, and Blue swept the field, rescuing every nation *ever*, because "fuck yeah, we did—we're badass."

I'm almost sorry to do this because I hate bursting creative bubbles, but in this case the truth needs to be said. Yes, our country was invaluable in helping both war efforts, and without our assistance those conflicts might have gone on for god knows how long. But we weren't the saviors of the planet; we did our part. We did what was necessary to try to ensure freedom in the world where it was welcomed. Yet so many other countries were instrumental in doing so as well. If you need more proof we're not that picture you've painted in your head, take a gander back over your shoulder at the messes that were the Korean and Vietnam conflicts. Shit didn't stack up in our favor on those. So everybody settle down on this whole "back-to-back world war champions" horseshit.

Another misconception, in my opinion, is that with the exception of the "terrorist countries" (not my words), the rest of the world loves us and really looks forward to our visits. Sure, there are some countries who dig us, and even some of the places where we're not exactly hugged upon landing will still treat us with a certain modicum of respect because they know that despite our loudness and rudeness, we'll spend money on all kinds of dumb shit. That is right around where the hospitality ends, though. Perhaps that's the way it needs to be, and why not, really? We have a knack for treating the world like a rug for our dirty boots. I've seen with my own eyes the way American tourists treat people. Wait staff are largely made to feel like slaves. Anyone who can't fill a simple request gets the silent treatment while also bellowing for "a manager who understands what the *fuck* I am saying!" I've seen grown adults throw plates of food on restaurant floors all because one slight thing was wrong, all while loudly proclaiming, "I will *not* be paying for that!" Basically, we're all the worst caricatures imaginable when it comes to what we think we can and will do. If you don't believe me, just remember it's going to be a while before people in Rio trust tourists in their bathrooms.

It's even worse when the people acting the most foolish are a part of the party you're with yourself. I do my best to keep them in check, but most other people don't, which frustrates the pure shit out of me. Would you let someone like that act that way in the States? No, FUCK NO, actually, and neither would local shopkeepers and owners. But that's different—it's domestic. Those owners know they'll kick your ass out in a speeding frog's heartbeat if you get your cock out of whack with them. Overseas it's a little different. In most places tourism is the biggest source of income—what's more, some of these cheese dicks know it too. So they take advantage of the hesitation because they know they have all of these poor merchants bent over a burning barrel. Why in the hell would we do that? Is it because we unconsciously think that's what tourists and refugees do in *our* country? Is it retaliation for the "immigrant fear"? Do we reverse a perceived behavior, even if that behavior is an invented lie? Why would we spend the money, fly, check in, and go out and about just to play the role of stereotypical ass-hat American who has no chill whatsoever?

Maybe it's because we don't know how to act anywhere that may or may not have an abundance of freedom. So subconsciously we act up in a way to "rebel" for people around us who "can't." I know, that sounds like a fucking cop-out, but honestly, I'm just spit-balling in an attempt to come to some other conclusion than "it's because we fucking suck at almost everything." There it is: I said the very thing I was trying so hard not to say. You, my kind and earnest reader, may not want to admit this to yourself, but brace yourself: being American doesn't automatically make you awesome at everything. That may be what they teach us in our indoctrination—that is, school, TV, magazines, propaganda, and so forth—but that's a sad fact of life. Yes, we hit the geographical jackpot when we were born here or, if you emigrated, came to the democratic version of the biggest and best mall in the whole fucking world. For the most part it's fucking *awesome* here, and I wouldn't change all that good shit for all the money in all the world. But just because we're born American or work to become American, that doesn't mean that the first time we step outside our borders we can act the fucking fool.

Besides, it's getting quite close to the point where we won't be welcome in most places anymore anyway. The Cheeto keeps burning international bridges to find better spots for his fucking hotels and golf courses so we may be verboten in some of my favorite countries before you know it. The thought of not being able to go out into the world, whether as a visitor or a performer, really fucking depresses me. I am a vagabond spirit by nature, a restless traveler who only appreciates home when he's tasted the air in different lands, broken bread at civil faraway tables, and picked the grit from distant roads from my shoes so as to not trample dirt onto clean kitchen floors. I live to learn new words and phrases and to experience the flavors of a thousand new foods in a million old countries. If I have truly been back and forth and reincarnated, this may be the only life I know where most of my giant blue-green marble is off limits, even if my intentions are innocent and my eyes soft. That is not how we bring the world together. Shit, that's not even how you get *yourself* together. You'd never get to see the basilicas (or the only standing public statue of Satan—true story) in Spain. You'd never get to feel the wind whipping through the countryside of Great Britain. You'd never stroll the halls and smell the history of the galleries in France. You'd never feel the sand in your toes as you walk the dunes, looking at pyramids in Egypt or even the pyramids in Mexico or the other countries in South America. You'd never know the thrill of getting your first glimpses of Mt. Fuji as you speed on the bullet train in Japan. You'd never know the excitement of knowing—TRULY KNOWING—that those memories and sensations, while possibly familiar to other people, will *never* be identical to anyone else's memories. Those moments are yours and only yours. These are your life's fingerprints, splayed out before you, tracing the history of who we were, a gentle yet powerful reminder of our identity when we find ourselves lost in the battle between culture and history. This touchstone makes it easier to find our gravitas before we succumb to the gravity of any given situation outside our control.

That may be another great reason why people tend to let their basest rudeness take over when they are far from home: they simply don't know any better. It could be the way they were brought up—or lack thereof—or it could be a defense mechanism; I mean, I refuse to think that all people are fucked up. I cannot allow myself to give over to the assumption that just because you hail from the fifty nifty United States, that means you're going to be a three-hundred-pound shit-heel in a soggy sack of suck-ass while you trot around the globe. Does that make me the hopeless romantic? Or am I simply in love with the romance of hope? Hell, I've been called worse. I've been heckled on both sides of the aisle by people who claim to follow Jesus *and* Buddha. I think maybe I'm just too metal for their negative magnetism. Oh please, make no mistake: I don't have any plans to change my shit. Those people can take turns swinging from the undercarriage while they scrape the barnacles from my nuts. While they're at it, they can pick that shit up and eat it for all I care. The point is that the best way to enjoy the world and all your travels is to know who you are first. If you're still an uninterested spectator in your own life, how the hell are you going to enjoy being a spectator to the millions of resources this world has to offer? That shit, on its big, fat, moon-shaped face, just doesn't make any fucking sense.

There are places in the world where we are not welcome, this is true. There are spots on the map where the very thought of our existence is an insult to their way of life. I know that makes a lot of people nervous, but it shouldn't. The simple matter is this has *always* been the case. The whole world is not going to love America, and historically, the whole world hasn't. Ever since our inception there have been countries aligned against our interests. Such is life, to be fair. It's like having a big group of friends. Chances are very great that at least two people in that group are not going to totally get along. Along those same lines, there are very good odds that not everyone will like *you*—there may be friends of friends who hate your fucking guts. This is just human nature. Now, on a national level, there are certainly regions of our own country that do not get along. So why would we expect the rest of the world to get along with us or even be our friends? I'm quite sure the only reason some of these countries talk to us is because if they didn't we'd blow them the fuck out of whatever ocean they happened to be surrounded by, watching them sink below the waves as we whistled "Dixie." Yes, we're fucking dicks sometimes. We'll get into that a little more later when we talk about foreign policy and shit like that, but it's the truth. Just because you're the toughest kid on the playground doesn't mean you get an automatic invitation to everyone's birthday parties.

I was a latecomer to the whole "traveling abroad" thing. I didn't even get on a plane until I was twenty-three, and that was because I was flying to Great Britain to make an appearance on my friend Stella Katsoudas's first major label release, which she was recording at Peter Gabriel's studio in Bath, about two hours outside of London. This was way before Slipknot was even a thing. To the people making her album, I was merely "some kid from Iowa she insists be on the album with her." I'd been all over the United States as well as to Canada and to Tijuana when I was five, but I'd never left my terra firma, so to speak. I was quite excited but scared to death at the same time. This was years before 9/11, so things were more lax than they are now. I rolled onto the plane in steel-toed boots, a trench coat, dread locks, and a damn knife I forgot was in my backpack when I left. After some stares in my direction when we were delayed for "security reasons," we took off, landing late into London Heathrow Airport. Little did I know that I was about to have a really shitty afternoon.

I was told that when I landed I was to look for a driver who would be holding a sign saying, "Taylor—Studio." I was sort of chanting that as I made the arduous journey known as "trying to get the fuck out of Heathrow Airport." You may laugh, but anyone who's been there knows it's no fucking laughing matter. There are corridors that stretch on for fucking kilometers (we're talking about the UK, after all), and twists and turns and roundabouts that will make you ready to punch a nun in the fucking face just to get to an exit. That's all just trying to find Customs. Then it's another goddamn sojourn to get to baggage claim. Then the final three kilometers are the hallway just to get to the outside lobby—*not* the outside itself, but the outside lobby. So basically it takes what feels like a week just to taste fresh air (or, in my case, to finally have a cigarette), and by the time I hit the outside lobby I was ready to fight, fuck, or flee. Then I remembered what I was supposed to look for: Taylor—Studio. I cast my eyes around and saw a kindly man with graying red hair holding that very sign. I sauntered over and assured him that I was the man he was looking for. He smiled nicely and introduced himself as Harry, sort of surprised. "Oh good," he said. "You're quite early!" Seeing as I was in fact late by thirty minutes, that should have been my first clue that I was making a mistake. But I said fuck it and followed him out to his car, searching for a quiet place to have a smoke.

We packed up the standard-issue black sedan with my belongings and proceeded to leave the airport. We began talking a lot, and Harry began telling me all about the background of some of the places we were seeing, like the British Museum of Natural History, which is held in the building that used to house the Bedlam Hospital for the Criminally Insane, or so he claimed. Anyway, we'd been in the car about forty-five minutes when, in the course of our discussions, it became clear that, much to my chagrin, I was in the wrong fucking car. It turned out I should have been looking for more specifics on my own driver's sign: I was to look for a sign that said, "Corey Taylor—Big Fish Studios." Harry was looking for a Sean Taylor, to take him to BBC Studios. When we figured it out, we both laughed for a second, then got stuck because we weren't sure what to do next. These were the days before cell phones (or at least before they were practical and affordable), and I had no way of getting ahold of anyone. So the only thing I could think to do was have Harry drop me off at the offices of Stella's record label so I could try to get ahold of someone connected to her management or production team. To be honest, the rest of it was kind of a blur because I was so fucking jet-lagged that I passed out on the couch in their waiting room, only waking up to give them information. After I had bid farewell to Harry and wished him luck on his own trip back to find Sean Taylor, I sat and waited for my own driver to pick me up. After a few hours he arrived, and we made off for beautiful Bath, named because of the natural springs that served as a spa and baths for royalty and the upper crust in ages gone by. That is a place I'd very much like to go back to someday.

Now, if I'd been a normal asinine American traveler, these people might have left me to rot. As it stood, even at twenty-three and miles from home, I knew enough to keep my shit together and remain calm. I didn't go ape shit Kong style and freak out on these poor people who had nothing to do with the actual fuck-up in the first place. And I'd like to think that because I was calm and gracious, they really went above and beyond to help this crazy-looking kid get out to Peter Gabriel's studio. I've never forgotten that kindness, and I hope all the people who helped me went on to get knighted or damed or whatever they do for damn fine people over there. I'm a full-on Anglophile—you'd think I'd know this sort of thing. Nevertheless, I still think it was because of my demeanor that I could get such wonderful help.

Let me wrap this up like this: stop treating the rest of the world like a fucking Mardi Gras kegger or a wet T-shirt contest on South Padre Island. If you want to do that shit, do it here—it's very accepted here. Better yet, if you feel the need to do it abroad, do it in places like Spain or France where they have all-night dances or at the summer festivals in Germany where the rave tents will give even the most hardened partier a run for their money. Do what you want—I'm not gonna judge you too harshly. You're American after all, which means you come with a certain set of disadvantages anyway. But do yourself—and every weary traveling tourist after you—a solid favor. No, don't start bitching yet—just fucking listen. You want people to get back to thinking that America is the greatest country in the world? Then start acting like it. Good winners don't rub that shit in other people's faces. They're solid on the inside; they don't need that self-aggrandizing hullabaloo. Real winners demonstrate the culture they represent and encourage others to emulate it by making it attractive and appealing. Winners don't bark orders at tired wait staff; winners offer assurances that any help they can provide will be fully appreciated. Winners don't shit on cultures or places that fill their citizens with national pride; winners add their own praise and spread the word about the wonders of these locales. Winners don't act like fucking cunts on a day pass; they're too busy trying to make sure the people around them are as fulfilled as they are. That's what winners do. They don't try to take the piss out of a foreign community by insulting it. They raise a glass in a happy toast of appreciation.

I'd like to think we used to be a society that did that for our neighbors, domestic and abroad. I'd like to. There's a part of me that wonders whether we've always had a little too much "angry oppressor" in us to truly enjoy another's cultures. That's why we try to be better hosts than visitors. We all try to be more at home—well, at home, really. But only someone at peace with him or herself can truly see their surroundings as more than a backdrop for their own theatrical tragedy. The second we forget we're all connected to this planet, cut from the same cosmic cloth, is when the very molecules become the bars of our metaphysical prison. No matter where we go, how loud we try to get, or how selfish we treat our fellow brothers and sisters on this fruited plain, in the end it all comes clean for better or for worse. Dirty laundry can be a burden if you let it build up too long, and if you don't take a second to listen to and, ultimately, understand the various voices all around us, you'll never realize that some of those voices could be offering you that help you so desperately crave in life. So if you go on "walkabout" or holiday or just plain-old vacation, treat that country the same way your parents *should* have taught you to treat a stranger's house: with respect and kindness. Wipe your feet, take off your shoes, and for god's sake, don't clog up the fucking toilets.

CHAPTER 8

RULE AMERICANA

I HAVE LONG BEEN A FAN OF HISTORY—NOT A STUDENT, but a *fan*. I've read so many books that I might have carcinogens from library dust. I've watched documentaries until my eyes have turned Technicolor. I have dragged my family to so many battlefields and historic "points of interest" that they now check around potential vacation spots to make sure I can't take them anywhere that is—and this is quoting my niece, by the way—"boring as whale shit and smells like an old church." So yes, I am a *fan* of history because I am a fan of stories in general, and what is history really except the stories from the past, ready and willing to help us shape our future? I mean ye gads (I never get to say that), it's in the damn *name itself!* HI-STORY! Where are we without it? What do we do without it? What happens when we forget the lessons it has tried to show us? Even as a fan of history, I have always tried to temper my enthusiasm for our past with a respect for the tragedies it has beheld as well, realizing that death and loss have always gone hand-in-hand with life and victory. They say, "to the victor, the spoils"; I say, "to the savvy, the subtleties."

So you'll understand the conflict within me when, many moons ago, I found myself walking slowly and reverentially through the quiet of the monuments and the museum at Dachau, just outside Munich, a fairly intense experience whether or not you know its full history. The sprawl covers lots of ground. Most of the structures have been razed to the ground, but pictorials and video show how it was laid out, including a re-creation of one of the "bunkhouses," which was really just a glorified trailer where, sadly, they kept too many people in such a space. Out of respect for the dead I won't go into too much detail. But I will tell you that it was a haunting and enlightening moment for me. The only thing that kept me from truly crumbling under the sheer emotional weight of it all was that in our way, America helped stop the human evil responsible for this historical trauma. I don't normally get all patriotic or "Lee Greenwood" or any of that corny shit, but knowing that my country helped stop an overwhelming wave of fascism made me proud, if even for a second. The meaning of this place was clear: NEVER FORGET THE PAST, OR YOU WILL BE DOOMED TO RELIVE IT. DON'T IGNORE HISTORY, OR YOU WILL BE DOOMED TO REPEAT IT. What happened to the Jewish people in this place and others like it is one of the most vile atrocities to happen in the history of humanity. Even with the mistakes we've made in the United States, we've managed to stand for something while also standing against that type of barbaric hate.

If only we'd held on to that righteous feeling . . .

This country has a crazy up-and-down love affair with taking massive shits in other people's backyards. The fucked-up thing is that we were *never* supposed to be this way. We were the global isolationists, really only joining conflicts at the very last minute and only then really because our own country was being threatened or attacked. We would stay away and stay away, holding on until we just couldn't hold back anymore. We just loved to mind our own business. Now, however, we can't really keep our snouts out of the trough. We strapped ourselves to a fucking Roman candle and tried to become the latest in a long line of that candle's namesake's conquerors. Under the guise of being the "world police" or the "sheriffs of Earth," we instead fell headfirst down a rabbit hole full of oil, money, and nefarious self-interest. Invasion became the name of the game, all while stuffing fistfuls of bullshit into the propaganda meat grinder: "fighting communism," "fighting drug trafficking," "fighting guerrilla fighters," "fighting terrorism," "fighting zealots" . . . the infinite loop closes behind us as we find ourselves devoted to an ideal that isn't true, which does wonders for our international appeal, to be honest.

Now, before I go any further, let's get something straight: this is *not* about our military. I am not making this point because I have anything against our current servicemen and -women, nor do I have anything against former veterans. As a matter of fact, members of my family have served our military going back before my grandfather, who served in Korea. I support every man and woman who has fought and died or stood with our military, no matter where they are. No, what I'm going to talk about is *policy*. These people join our various armed forces to be a part of something that has honor and takes courage. They can't help what these chicken-shit politicians stir up, nor can they help what they are forced to defend from time to time. Soldiers care about country and family—two things the government lets get lost in the shuffle all too often because of ego or conflict of interest. So when I talk about the certain invasions and subsequent evasions that have happened and inevitably will happen again, I'm not talking about my family and friends following orders and their hearts; I'm talking about the dicks behind the desks who, with one loss of temper, can flare up, rise up, and fuck up everyone's holidays, leading to loss of perspective and, more importantly, life.

Maybe it's because we caught empire fever. That could be the reason we hold our hands over our hearts for the pledge of allegiance and "The Star-Spangled Banner": because that's what the Romans did as well when they did their salute. That could be why we've tried to hold onto all these US territories like Puerto Rico and the Virgin Islands: because that's what our "ex-benefactors," the British, did right up until the end of World War II. That could be a subconscious reason we were so against the Germans and why we still have issues with the Russians: because we've bullshitted ourselves into thinking that because we're "good" and "righteous" and "fight for freedom," we're the only ones allowed to pursue international land holdings (aka, to just bully in and declare some random place is "American-held land"). That last example is what we've done with our "word of mouth," and we'll talk about that a little more later. I'll be honest: that word of mouth hasn't held well. That only works now inside our own country. The rest of the world is on to us—as the movies love to say, "The jig is up, Sharky!" We can't play that conquest-disguised-as-liberation card anymore. We used to be the journeymen; now we're the bogeymen.

Is that our legacy, our lot in this life? Were we doomed to become the very thing we claimed to be fighting against? Sometimes I wonder if the United States from the 1900s had a better idea of what needed to be done. Even Woodrow Wilson couldn't keep us out of the Great War, but at least at first we were adamant about staying out of foreign conflict. Isolationism doesn't solve *all* the problems; we are, in fact, a large part of a huge global community, and we do need to have a presence in it. People look to us for answers, so getting involved is only natural. We can't stay out of everything. However, we *do* need to pay a little more attention to what's on our side of the fence. By doing that, I do *not* mean "building a fucking wall" or deporting immigrants from countries that present no threat whatsoever. I mean setting up programs specifically designed to decelerate drug use and unemployment in lower-income cities, counties, and states. I mean using funds for good, not bad. I can already *hear* the conservatives out there bitching that "tax money can't go to pay for that." Well, guess what, bitches: Would you rather your tax money go to help our fellow Americans or to build a pointless wall that isn't going to keep *anyone* out? Not one fucking person is going to be kept out of the United States of America because of that fucking wall. If you're dumb enough to believe *that* border is the *only* way to get into this country, you may want to look at a fucking map. We have oceans on both sides—are you going to build a wall all the way down the coasts? We also have a *giant* country above us—are you going to build some shit up there? All of that "build a wall" horseshit is fine and dandy when you're getting morons and racists worked up to vote for you, but when it comes to practical application, that shit just isn't fucking cricket. It's a lot like that show *Finding Bigfoot*: they haven't *found* shit. It should be called *Looking for Bigfoot*, but no one wants to watch someone who's just looking for that critter. The trick is in the promise, not the delivery.

Sorry if I pissed anyone off with that little blast at the end there. I'm probably one of the few people in this country who *enjoys* being able to go abroad. It's a little too tense (two tents) for my comfort anymore, but I honestly don't have a choice—I have to tour to make money. I also really fucking like playing for people all over the world. So I have to balance the coolness of the show with the obvious high levels of snark that accompany my arrival anywhere outside the shows. After all these years I'm used to it—it just means I don't go out as much when I'm on the road. It's fine. It saves me from being judged all the damn time for some shit I'm so clearly against. But it's also one of the reasons why, unless you *need* to show your passport, the aforementioned "Canadian camouflage" works so well to defuse any animosity or disdain that may fly your way once they pin the vanilla accent. I'm sure my northern brothers and sisters will find that either funny or offensive, but hell, how do you think I feel? If I have to say "aboot" and "eh" a couple of times to keep my food from getting soaked in foreign spit, that's what I'm going to talk aboot, eh? I won't be sorry for doing whatever is necessary to keep myself from contracting international Hepatitis A, B, and C. That's one fucking test I never want to ace, *ever*.

When I talk foreign policy, I *do* always forget about our northern and southern neighbors, but I can't really do that anymore these days, with the Cheeto threatening anyone slightly or completely brown with annihilation or, worse yet, throwing veiled shade their way so his shitty base takes the hint and does the threatening for him. Cunty moves like that make me really fucking stabby. In fact, I can hardly wait until I'm done with this fucking book so I can keep from driving myself crazy with all the nightmare scenarios he's thrust upon us because of his ego and cluelessness. People gave him great marks for his first address to Congress just because he didn't say anything *too* inflammatory. You've got to be fucking kidding me. Adults would have laughed this fucking mook out into the goddamn hallway years ago. But because the Right is so ravenous and the Left is so flaky and lame, we're stuck with a man who thinks we can outmuscle foreign opposition by piling up nuclear weapons like he's sending dick picks to employees, with the clear insinuation that if he doesn't get what he wants, all his penises are going to shoot at once. Death by cock envy—god, isn't it a great time to be alive . . .

Anyway, thank god, there's people like Trudeau keeping watch on the crazy downstairs neighbor. Sometimes all you need to do to keep dumb shit in check is have a dude who looks like he could rip your fucking head off in a fight. It doesn't hurt that Trudeau's easy on the eyes too. I figure if he comes to a gig and I happen to have my Canadian *Teen Beat* with him on the cover, he'll sign it. I might even have a shot, you know? I'd climb that man like a water tower in a city on fire. I feel like the more I write here, the more you're all getting uncomfortable with the thought of me actually daydreaming about the prime minister of Canada. That's not *my* fault; that's *your* fault. I'm comfortable enough to imagine myself riding on the back of a jet ski with Justin Trudeau, smiling and happy, water cascading all around us, both slightly oily from the Coppertone we generously applied to each other's . . . okay, maybe I am putting a little too much thought into this whole "I Heart Trudeau" scenario, but it's only because he hasn't replied to me on Twitter. As soon as he replies to me on Twitter, I'll be able to move on. I mean, I knit him a sweater and fucking everything! What does a guy have to do to get noticed by the head of a major country's government these days? Pose nude? Well, I'm not doing *that* . . . again . . .

Sorry, where was I?

The first time I can remember hearing about "combative foreign policy" was when I was thirteen or fourteen, and the big news was the Iran-Contra affair, a sort of paramilitary shell game that became the albatross around the necks of the entire Reagan administration. Even though we weren't technically pushing into a foreign territory, we *were* trying to obfuscate from obeying the laws and regulations set up by Congress against (1) selling arms to Iran, and (2) continuing to fund the rebels known as the Contras in Nicaragua. Ostensibly under the guise of freeing hostages held by Hezbollah in Lebanon, a triad of payments and favors was devised behind the government's back, largely put together by those inside Reagan's inner circle. It's still not really clear how much ol' Dutch really knew about the complexities of the operation itself, but he and Lieutenant Colonel Oliver North both fell on the sword, so to speak, accepting the lion's share of the blame. I can remember several news stories and a million different songs written by everyone from Don Henley to Dave Mustaine talking about the whole scandal in detail. I was confused, then intrigued, and then finally started studying politics and all the implications that come from that sort of behind-the-scenes shenanigans. Far from the back-channel diplomacy of years gone by, it was a scary time and another knock to the shiny apple used in our American pies.

But it also showed me that no matter the outrage, no matter the fallout, and no matter the level of controversy, these politicians *walked*. The last high-level motherfucker to really ever feel the sting of the law was Nixon, and even *he* was allowed to resign and split, later to be pardoned by Gerald Ford. This would apparently set the precedent: from Clinton and his blowjobs to the Cheeto and whatever the hell is going on with the Russian connection, the threat of prosecution rarely goes any further than just that—threats. Maybe that's why Trump's not worried about anything actually happening. So he can piss on foreign relations all the livelong day and never break a sweat while he waves his egomaniacal cluster of nuclear cocks at the entire world. You know . . . because 'Murica.

I apologize to anyone masturbating at this moment while screaming 'Murica, by the way.

Our hypocritical handle on the global arena is summed up, like I said, by the fact that we outwardly abhor that type of empirical attitude and yet we have territories that are subject to our laws but get none of our benefits as a capitalist-pig nation. Take, for example, Puerto Rico. It is technically an "unincorporated territory," which implies that it is on its way to statehood, and yet nothing has been done for 114 years to change its status, largely because the territorial laws and policies have never been defined, allowing the territory to be taken advantage of and leaving millions of potential US citizens to be marginalized and exploited, along with Puerto Rico itself. The laws here in America do not apply to citizens in places like Puerto Rico, so it's a lot like the Wild West. Imagine being a native of Puerto Rico, having to abide by US law to an extent, but then having to deal with a bunch of naturalized cocksuckers who just want to get away with murder or at least date rape between barhops. You know why? Because Americans tend to become evil bastards when they cross our outer borders. I won't get off on that crazy asshole rant—we covered that in the last chapter. You should've read it before this one, unless you skipped it, hoping that the nudes were in *this* chapter. Well, they're not. I'll be honest, I'm fairly certain they leaked to the Internet before I could include them in the packaging for the book. There's not much to talk about, so I'll sum it up by saying yes, that's it; no, it's not huge; thank you, it *is* quite thick.

In the last twenty years we've decided that our main priority is to clear all the shit from the sandbox, so to speak, so most of our foreign conflicts have taken place in the oldest parts of civilization on Planet Earth. I'd acquiesce to the fact that it's important for us to try to stop ISIS from not only killing thousands of people but also halt their unbelievable destruction of some of the holiest and most ancient structures, monuments, and buildings history has ever seen. The obscenity of their disdain for everything around them is truly disgusting. However—and you *might* not like this—if we hadn't been fucking around in that region in the first place, we wouldn't fucking be in this situation. We were working with the Taliban—YES, THE FUCKING TALIBAN—in the eighties when we were trying to help them repel the Russians from Afghanistan and other areas. Plus, while working with Saddam Hussein—YES, SADDAM FUCKING HUSSEIN—to control some of the more violent and religious movements, we helped him secure his secular government and, thereby, his stranglehold on Iraq. Then we got wrapped up in the region, the Taliban became our enemy, we attacked Hussein because "oil," and all of a sudden the United States was officially the Big, Bad Oppressor all over Africa, not just to Khomeini and Gaddafi but to every tribal or government leader around. Yay! We did it!

I don't want people to think I'm insinuating that we deserved the terrorist attacks that have happened to us. I also don't want to make it sound like there weren't threats that needed to be dealt with; some of those extremists, bin Laden included, would have done terrible things to other places even if they hadn't come after us. However, my point is simple: there were other ways for us to help those people, but maybe certain heads of our government balanced the effects of meddling in the region with the benefits and access to all the petroleum, and they threw almost all caution to the wind. So you'd *think* that some political bites to the national ass would get us to realign our priorities and straighten out the bottom line. Yeah, not really: we're just casting about looking for other places to set up our fucking lethal erector sets. Hell, Trump's even indicated that he will ostracize or reward those countries that won't play ball with him and "The Trump Brand": like those hotels, golf courses, bacon bowls (maybe not), piano ties (also can't back that up), and whatever the fuck Ivanka shills for Macy's, or Target, or wherever the fuck she shills whatever the fuck she shills. Get the picture? Good, at least someone does. I'm *totally* lost . . .

An interesting side effect of this world-trampling warmongering is the paranoia that happens stateside. All through the Cheeto's campaign he kept *assuring* Americans that we were in danger from international terrorists and illegal immigrant criminals. While the former has its truth in smaller doses, neither of them are *nearly* the threat he would lead us to fucking believe. In fact, since 9/11 more people in this country have been killed by domestic *Caucasian* terrorists than by international threats—a statistic that glares in the face of everything these hateful cunts want to push on us. But to *them*, a fucking immigration ban (read: "anyone not *really* white" ban) makes total sense when they're slinging around this shitty rhetoric. Fear is the stick shift on the Ferrari of control: the higher the gear, the higher the revs and the bigger the boost out of the gate. So of course the Trump administration is going to use "fake news" sites like Breitbart to ramp up and justify policies that make Americans *feel* safe. But what's going to happen when other countries start banning Americans from coming into their worlds with our hateful entitlement? They don't *have* to let us in either. We just assume, because we're the great white global sheriffs, that other countries are happy to see us and welcome us in with open arms. My experience is quite the opposite: lots of times our very presence in another country or our association with their government makes them a target. So why the hell would anyone want to hang out with or invite over the kid in school who *always* makes a scene and breaks shit at the party? We're America; we're fucking assholes. If I were the head of a foreign government, I'd probably keep my fucking distance. Thus, I think sooner rather than later, while this shithead administration is busy banning other countries (read: colors) from coming into our own, more and more countries are going to do the same thing to us. The shitty part is that we'll deserve it.

If you don't believe me, let me tell you the old tale of the American Who Had Too Many Irish Car Bombs.

The year was 2001. The place was Paris, France. Slipknot had just played an incredibly successful concert at the Zenith. Beforehand we'd made our by-now traditional sojourn to "see Jim," visiting Morrison's grave at Père Lachaise and leaving him an all-access pass. After the show we didn't have to go anywhere very quickly, so a decision had to be made: go on to the next city (in Germany, I believe) or stay in Paris and go absolutely fucking bonkers running around the Party Vous Francais. Of course we opted for the latter choice, and we all scattered like spores on the cross breezes, looking for the darkest kinds of trouble imaginable. This dispersal led to revelations about glitter discos, burning bathrooms, and finding a tall gentleman passed out *standing up* in an elevator. But for me, I slid sideways through the din and went in search of my own insane form of refreshment. Our tour bus was parked on a two-lane one-way near a park boxed in by concrete and traffic on all sides, but cosmopolitan company was just around the corner, so I split from the skids and just kept turning corners until I found where I was supposed to be. It was a bit chilly, but I was already fairly tipsy at that point—plus, I was fat, hairy, and covered in layers. With this in mind, I unleashed myself on an unsuspecting French public.

About two hours later I woke up. It took me a second to realize where the hell I was. I had the vaguest of recollections about wandering into an Irish pub—in France, I know—and propping myself up at the bar. As this was occurring to me, I noticed the mess around my feet and the look of horror in the sparse number of patrons sitting ALL THE WAY ON THE OTHER SIDE of the pub. The barkeep had a towel over his arm and a scowl on his face. I was reaching the conclusion that I wasn't welcome there. I would have left right away, but I also kind of wanted to know what I'd done. Yeah, for some reason this FUBAR sense of attrition came over me, and I suddenly wanted to apologize for whatever it was that I'd done. I tried to stand up and lean over the bar to speak to the bartender, who was still grimacing at me, but my legs had suddenly turned into a pair of gelatinous stumps, like two pillowcases filled with pudding instead of the foundation for my shitty body. I clutched at the wood of the bar to steady myself, and for a split second I saw the *slightest* smirk come across the bartender's face, and he relaxed for a minute. When he relaxed the rest of the bar did as well. That allowed me to get my collective smack together.

Once I knew he would listen to me, I barely mumbled, "I'm so sorry if I've offended anyone here tonight." It was the worst slurred speech *ever*. But apparently the bartender was fluent in dickish drunk, because he simply shook his head and waved his hand as if to say, "C'est la vie." Satisfied, I made as if to leave. But he called me back: "Monsieur, excuse me." He came around the bar to stand next to me. "I understand you're . . . sick," he made a vomiting face, and I gave him a laugh in turn. Then he got serious. "But I'm afraid you need to settle your bill before you go home." I was quite apologetic and asked what the tab was. He smiled and said, "three hundred francs." It didn't quite click with me for a second, then it hit me. Three hundred fucking francs?! That was about the same total in American dollars at the time. How the fuck did I spend basically three hundred bucks *by myself?* I came to find out that I drank eight Irish car bombs, which is a shot of Jameson mixed with Bailey's, then dropped into a pint of Guinness, depth-charge style, and chugged as fast as you possibly can before the Bailey's curdles. I know what you're thinking, and yes, it *is* fucking delicious. Now eight car bombs don't come to three hundred bucks. But apparently I was spitting beer and whiskey at the people around me as well, so every time I'd order a drink, the barkeep ordered one for the people in the bar as well—on me. I opened my mouth to say something about that being some prime-time bullshit, and then suddenly I just nodded. I got it—I'd been a complete cunt. I wasn't nearly as bad as Dick was in Japan, but I was pretty bad, and I deserved it. So I ran my credit card and split.

Now imagine *every* American tourist doing that every night but not eating the crow when they get the payback. Imagine having to deal with that on every level, all the fucking time because people from all over the world come to your country as tourists but decide to *not* behave as if they're in their own country. Now imagine those tourists are military. Now imagine that they don't leave, *ever*. Sometimes an absurd idea like the one I just presented doesn't seem too crazy when you think about the fact that it does happen a little too often. Don't believe me? Ask Iraq. We overstay our welcome all the time, like I did in the bar. I'm sure that dude couldn't *wait* to get rid of me, even after making sure I paid my bill. To wrap *that* story up, after I left the bar I eventually succumbed to the drunken munchies and found a storefront restaurant selling chili dogs stuffed with French fries—which is a truly nutritious and balanced meal to have at 3:30 in the fucking morning. I went back to the bus, laid down in the back lounge, and woke up puking. It was *everywhere.* It took me forever to clean up on my own, and the smell never really went away. Boom went the dynamite, all over Uncle Fuckmouth's nice tour bus. If only our national karma could suffer through some of that so we'd learn our lessons.

Look, I know most Americans don't want the United States nosing around in other countries' affairs, instead yearning for a time when we look more to our own bullshit than raking up stink in barns that don't belong to us. No, I didn't hear that anywhere; I came up with that saying on my own. I feel like it's pretty fitting: we do need to stop fucking around in other people's yards and pay a little more attention to what's up in our own house. The problem with that is we the people have very little to do with when, how, and why that happens in the first place. Between the lobbyists and the politicians who ultimately get us into this shit, no one really asks us what *we* think. They give us just enough info to get our blood up by showing us front-loaded news stories to control our bias, then they slip into conflicts around the world based on whatever their interests are at the time. We as Americans, if hard pressed, are largely in favor of letting the world get on with its own shit while we do our own thing. There's *nothing* wrong with that, by the way. It's actually healthier for the world when other countries figure out their own troubles. If we're solicited, I think it's cool if we, as a collective, help as a part of NATO. But unfortunately, our global reputation precedes us now. We can make or break a second chance for a third-world country. We can take or leave the best shot for a better future in the hands of people not really dedicated to something as positive as bolstering a foreign market or helping with things such as water supplies or medical facilities. Yes, there are independent organizations that handle that, but depending on the relations our government has with certain countries can also mean putting your life at risk for tribal violence or kidnapping. That's not me being a paranoid ass; that shit happens, and it shouldn't happen to good people who give up their lives to help others.

You all know I'm a first-class comic-book geek. I grew up reading the exploits of everyone from Spider-Man to Batman. I've always loved those characters, who they were, and what they stood for. But I'll tell you: a character I forgot I loved just as much as Spidey was Captain America. In fact, one of my favorite comics is a Spider-Man/Captain America crossover. I love Cap because he is the embodiment of what America was *supposed* to stand for: what is right and just, color-blind to race, and empathy and justice for all. Captain America was more than the spirit of the USA; he was a good man, one to aspire to being. To me, when I was growing up he was my impression of what America actually was. Maybe he's the whole reason I still have a pinch of patriotism in my blood. The thing I love most about the Cap in the comics is that, like me and a lot of Americans, he had that "crisis of faith" where he didn't recognize himself in the America he was looking at. I know some cynics have a lot of issues with the American Superhero being a blonde, blue-eyed man, but even Cap would tell you it's not about the *look* that's meant to be American—it's about who you *are*. There have been several attempts to update the character and even changing Steve Rogers himself, and every time I feel like they have failed because they forget what the character is supposed to be. Captain America is about the *ideal*, not the reality. That character is about the *hope*, not the hate. He's about the *promise*, no matter how many times the real world has allowed us all to break it. There are times when I curse Stan

Lee and Jack Kirby for giving us a character like Captain America; however, I'm secretly always happy they did. It's exactly this ideal that some of us look up to, to try to emulate, and to make us feel like we're not crazy for wanting to be more at peace than at war. There's nothing wrong with looking up to a fictional character's values. Nine times out of ten they are more real and sincere than most of these "family men and women" Republicans and Democrats, politicians who later get caught with hookers and blow while they spent most of their political careers gutting programs for families and taxing the shit out of working people. I'd rather have the beliefs of a comic book character than the values of a fucking lying thief.

To sum up this chapter is a tough one. There are some people like myself who feel that in order to improve our place in the world at large, we must slowly extricate ourselves from other countries' affairs in a manner that doesn't leave them in chaos. But there are others who believe we need to keep pushing into foreign territory, whether under the guise of "preserving international democracy" or "keeping the fascists and commies at bay with our very presence in an area." The dynamics don't really make sense when you figure that our global fingerprints are on a lot of shitty backfires and depressions. We label ourselves liberators, but in a lot of ways we only like the best bits of the action movies, so that's all we do: come in, start some shit, "free the people," and then split before the credits, unwilling to do the heavy labor because Americans only want stories about victories, not budgets and homework. To a lot of people the important part was the war or the fighting. That's not true: indigenous peoples always fight harder than liberators because there's more at fucking stake for them. They will gladly fight for themselves when the time comes. What they *really* need from us is the stability that comes with being a superpower (by the way, we gave ourselves that name, nobody else did). We should be there to help pick up the pieces, not blowing the shit out of everything in the first damn place. There's more good and a lot more karma in helping someone to their feet instead of pushing them down. The world has enough aggressors; what it truly needs are teachers, doctors, healers, and help.

I've had a philosophy in my life that has kept me on the straight and narrow for the last few years. Sure, it took me a few years and a whole lot of egotistical bullshit to figure it out, but once I did, I never forgot it: It only takes a few extra seconds to be nice to someone as opposed to being a screaming cock right out of the gate. You're not losing anything, you've given up nothing but a handful of important seconds and in the right situation, and you're also making someone' life by being nice. That person will spread that energy as long as it lasts, and the people they spread it to do the same, and so on and so forth, until your catalyst of goodness has tapped the pressure valves on real life and given people a temporary respite from the permanent pain in the ass that can be Life In Progress. To me there's no better reason to be that way than that right there. Some people get up in the morning, their experience is shit wall-to-wall, and then they go to bed with the taste of turds on their breath, no matter how many times they brush their teeth. The absolute bastard of it all is that they'll have to run that shit-stained gamut again when they wake up in the morning. So why not give them a break or make their day with some kindness, some coolness, a few extra seconds for a photo and some conversation? It's a good way to be—it doesn't *always* pay off, but it's not always about us, is it? Either way, the motivation is coming from a good place, and the afterglow can shine on crazy diamonds for a very long time if you do it right.

I feel like if America had that same mindset, we wouldn't be the Big, Bad Global Bully to a lot of nations. No nation is perfect, of course, but when you're the country who purports to have the most freedom and the most happiness, then you go setting fires and kicking over cans in other people's countries, that's what we call in the Taylor household a "dick move, Banner." There are a lot of nations who have us completely dialed and never ask us for a fucking thing because they know the tit-for-tat comes with a heavy bill, plus gratuity, plus interest, plus, plus, plus. We're the savages, the Vikings, the Huns, and the hoard on its way to Ford Theater. We are not so much the heroes of every story, but we're not the villain in each story either. It's complicated to say the least. It's like tiptoeing through minefields where even if you step on a landmine, they don't *all* kill you; some just pelt you with candy. But *you* don't know that, and you genuinely don't know which one is which. So proceed with caution, and glory comes with a nice "hallelujah" when you don't blow the shit out of yourself. Internationally, we're basically a Benny Hill skit, for fuck's sake. We're in a red-white-and-blue bikini, chasing all the other girls around because when we go down, we're taking everyone with us.

When I was walking the paths at Dachau, none of that was on my mind. I wasn't thinking about American mistakes or how the West was won. I was paying my respects to those who died for fascist, racist, hateful, horrible reasons. I was listening to the silence left behind in the wake of such an atrocity. I was letting that lesson sink in before feeling something as out of place as pride that the armed forces of the United States of America had something to do with liberating the survivors of this catastrophe. There was a fleeting thought about it, but I pushed it aside—it wouldn't have been right to feel that in that moment. I waited until I'd left to try to comprehend the dichotomy between the America that was, the America that is, and, worse yet, the America that certain leaders would have if given the opportunity. Today that thought process comes floating back across the stormy waters of my mind as I write this book, looking for the right wave, the perfect break, the point at which I should paddle out and surrender to the sea and all its metaphors for chaos theory. If you've ever wanted a more beautiful sense of poetry for what's happening in America today, look no further than our oceans. Yes, swirling below the surface is a world also made up of systems and routines, of life and all the things that come with life. Even if you find your place among it all, you could still be eaten alive in the blink of an eye.

When the curtain is pulled on this country, I don't want its legacy to be that of a roving predator in the deep blue sea. I want it to be more like the blue whale, making its way through the darkness, coming out to grab a breath every once in a while, but mainly doing its own thing, because anything and everything else is none of its business. It merely wants to live. Hopefully it breeds and passes life on to its children, but there's no guarantee of anything else. We must find a way to be that whale: concentrating more on our own place in the world and less on what others have gotten themselves into. Sometimes you have to let everyone else fail. But when you do, there's a very good chance that those same people will in fact win from losing. You have to come up off the mat sometimes to secure that knockout punch. Babies don't walk because we *want* them to, and they generally don't walk if we keep helping them all the time. They have to crawl, then stagger, then fall and cry, and then eventually climb to their feet under the strength of their own legs and take those first few faltering steps that will inevitably lead to walking, then running, then standing on their own. We must allow the world to do that; we can't afford the resentment that comes with holding their hands all the time and not allowing others to figure it out for themselves. Until we do that, we will not truly be a superpower or even a global leader. We'll simply become that asshole neighbor no one likes, who never minds their own business, constantly meddles in affairs that aren't their own, and by the end of the sitcom has been replaced with a less-aggravating actor or actress.

CHAPTER 9

CMFT + GOP = WTF

BEFORE YOU READ THIS CHAPTER I WANT YOU TO UNDERstand how difficult this is going to be for me to write. You see, although I may agree with some of the platforms and policies associated with the Republican Party, I have a hard time being fair and balanced with the GOP because, quite frankly, the people who abused me over the years held these same beliefs, even observing the hypocrisy of "family first" while beating the absolute shit out of me and tearing me down mentally and emotionally. I have come to equate my abusers with this party, largely because while my pain was going on, the Republicans were doing everything from debilitating the American farmer to performing voodoo economics on the public as a whole. The people I was living with and the others who allowed it to go on were—how do I put this delicately?—salt-of-the-earth-type folks. Professional alcoholics who lived paycheck to government check, unleashing their ignorant violence and drunken malice on children—these are *not* the overall view of who or what a Republican was, but for a long time that idea was all I had. Big, loud, forty-year-old adolescents who'd rather hit you than love you, all hopped up on whiskey, God, guns, and trucks. This was the better part of my childhood, if you could call it that. So I have to fight that stereotype when I go out on the high wire, letting my own bias get the better of my unabashed opinions and not-so-subtle way of pissing off the straights.

So I want you to comprehend this—*really* comprehend this—when I lay out today how much of the GOP platform I absolutely *do agree* with, and what's going to shock most of you is that there is actually a *lot* that I definitely do agree with. Things like the Second Amendment, the death penalty, lower taxes (for the middle class and downward, but we'll get to that), support for 98 percent of our law enforcement and our military, and, in a lot of ways, *smaller* government. Not that shit they're trying to shill right now under the guise of small government: deregulating everything yet sticking your fucking noses in people's business is *not* smaller government, you fucking tick-turds. I'm talking about *real* smaller government that allows local governments to do their jobs, on up through state governments and so on and so forth. Depending on how you felt about what I've written here so far, let's pretend for a second that I'm not Corey Taylor, the bigmouth fuck-face with a neck the size of a Yellowstone sequoia. Let's pretend I'm someone who digs most of the things I've been tearing apart. Let's pretend I'm, well, *you*, if you're running more with the elephants than the donkeys.

Yes, I am a firm supporter of *all* those platforms. I'm not saying they're all perfect. I'm not even saying they can't all be fixed in a way. But I *am* saying I am 100 percent behind these concepts. Why? Well, for one thing, I am a little more old school than some of you think, and I'd be lying if I said I was worried that you disagreed with me. And for another, crime and punishment are things deeply embedded in our national DNA, and I'm sorry, but some people have forgotten that. It needs to become a reminder. I'm no Buddhist; I'm a pragmatist. The only thing I have in common with the Big, Bald, Awesome Fat Guy is my belief in karma. I also back these ideas because they are connected to the original Constitution, which means they were put there for a reason. They were put there to keep despots from assuming power. They were put there to make sure we the people could protect ourselves. And although the times have changed and maybe our understanding of these rights may need updating, I still agree with them wholeheartedly. It may be because I was born and (mostly) raised in Iowa. It may be because most of my family is very conservative, and even though I've always been the rogue liberal, black-cat artist, I continue to agree on a lot of the things they are passionate about. Yes, I'm a city boy, through and through. But this city boy also used to do things like working "detassling" and driving tractors.

When I was a kid the only male role models I ever had were the washed-up, shitless, dick-breath dildos who blew through my mom's life from time to time. She dated some and befriended others. They were nothing special—essentially different fucked-up interpretations on similar crappy themes. Needless to say I never really learned anything substantial from any of these bleeding-gum mercs, with the exception of how to make a person pass out while holding them in the air or, oh yeah, also the proper angle to throw a plate at someone's face so as to break their nose but not the plate itself. So I didn't have a lot of great men to look up to in a lot of areas of my life. But the place where I *did* have great male role models was on my grandma's side of my family. I had several great aunts and uncles who were and still are very important to me. They instilled in me some values and work ethic—most of them ran their own farms. Before my life fell apart as a child, I have fond memories of spending time with all my cousins, having fun and being normal because they didn't care about my history or my bullshit—I was just family to them.

Back then the strongest man I'd ever known was my great-uncle Jim, or Uncle Jim for short. Uncle Jim was the father of my three closest cousins—Karl, Craig, and Todd—and we used to hang out every summer as much as we possibly could. So I got to see Jim a lot as a kid, and I'm telling you right now that in those days, he scared the *shit* out of me. Jim was a man's man: he worked for years at the Firestone plant until he retired, ran his own farm equipment, raced stock cars in Knoxville—I mean, Uncle Jim was the baddest motherfucker on the planet to me. I certainly didn't want to fuck with him. He had a way of raising his voice that I have tried to emulate with my own kids, just for the sheer terror it induced in me. By the way, I've never told him *any* of this, so if you're reading this, Jim, sorry, but you were pretty intimidating to this kid here. I loved all my uncles, but Uncle Jim was The Man.

By hanging out with the boys, I in turn learned how to be a boy myself. I learned how to ride go-carts and play sports. I learned how to stick to my chores and take responsibility for my actions. In fact, the very first time I touched a guitar was in their house. It only had four strings on it, and I don't even know if it was in tune, but that's where my love for the guitar began. So Uncle Jim and Aunt Sandy's house is where I saw how a working family works. Sure, it wasn't perfect, but they loved each other and still do. That was a house where I saw how a family lives and breathes. They had beliefs and faith and morals and a whole host of other things that I was bereft of; I may as well have been a feral kid. But in a lot of ways hanging out with Uncle Jim shaped the way I've tried to carry myself as a man and a father. He was the closest thing to a dad I ever had. I learned to respect and stand up for what I believe in, and that lesson has never been lost on me. We'll talk more about Uncle Jim later on—I just wanted to make sure you all met for a second. The reason I told you about my family is because when it comes to my conservative side, the side that has a very clear sense of right and wrong, no matter how fluid it might be, it comes from a place I care deeply about. This is not right-wing fanaticism flaring up; this is just a melding of the minds, the crossroads where liberal and conservative meet. Shall we begin?

Let's start with the death penalty, because to *me* it should be a no-brainer.

As far as I'm concerned, it's simple: you take a life in cold blood, we take yours. I'm truly sorry to some of you who feel it's harsh or inhumane or, worse yet, it's not a real deterrent for anything. That's a giant pile of horseshit. All you need to do is look at the facts. People may say that crime is going down, but the *violence* involved, the *viciousness* and pure *sadism* is going *up*. That's because there's no real threat of punishment, no worries about any sense of retribution. I'm not saying the death penalty would solve the whole problem, but a healthy death penalty would surely put some pause in a motherfucker's actions. If the threat of death were there, maybe they'd put away the knife or not load the gun. If the threat of death were there, maybe there wouldn't be so many white men running around killing minorities. I know that's not a very popular view among Republicans, but motherfuckers, the proof's in the shootings. These white domestic terrorists should face the strictest and harshest justice there is—I'm not a believer in saving all the crazy people to study them and learn from them. You want time to talk? Fine, you've got until their appeals run out. After that, these bastards fry for good. No more treating this with kid gloves, no more turning the other cheek, and no more rising above that sort of behavior. Guess what? We're humans. That means we're assholes. You hippies want to pretend we're better than all that vengeful stuff, you go right ahead. But as a survivor of domestic violence and as a man who's known and lost people to it, you'll find no mercy or peace from me. The world can be a brutal place; there need to be brutal consequences for people's actions or in no time at all the levels of violent entitlement will grow to the point of no return. There must be punishment. There must be justice, and god damnit, yes, there must be revenge.

There are some stipulations, of course. The death penalty doesn't apply to *any* nonviolent crime. Furthermore, if there isn't enough proof, it's off the table. There have been too many innocent people sent to prison because of bullshit pride, professional stubbornness, and outright prejudice or hate. The death penalty must be reserved for the worst of the worst, not those who may or may not be on the lines of guilt. That's where I stand on it—this is something I know comes down to a case-by-case basis, but it doesn't change the fact that it needs to be. It needs to *be*. It's like not disciplining your kids. Sure, there are exceptions where it sort of works, but the majority of the time those kids are fucking walking all over their parents, acting like assholes, and waving their bratty self-entitled bullshit around like an umbrella indoors. When it comes to the guilty—beyond-a-shadow-of-a-doubt guilty—there need to be ramifications for the damage done. Most of these killers and rapists and whatnot don't fear prison because they end up better off than they were on the street: a place to sleep, food, exercise, books, religion, education, better hygiene—these fuckers don't care about their "punishment." Only those who've been sent to a violent prison for a slight offense understand how bad prison is supposed to be. To the other alpha villains, it's just a giant cement clubhouse. Fuck that shit. To me, if you're a serial killer, you're dead. If you're a rapist, you're dead. If you're a violent criminal, you're dead. If you've harmed women, children, animals, the old or basically anyone else who can't defend themselves, you deserve to die. Fuck you and your second chances. I do believe in "innocent until proven guilty," but I also believe in "eye for an eye, tooth for a tooth, life for a life." Please don't ask me to apologize.

That's a perfect segue into law enforcement. I know there has been a rift in our country, coming long before I was around and coming on the heels of intolerable violence and cruelty toward American citizens, especially blacks, Hispanics, Native Americans, and Muslims. The actions of various law enforcement officers (LEOs) and the agencies they represent are unconscionable; they are supposed to protect and to serve, not to dominate and to repress. But I have faith that this is a small percentage; I've had the chance to meet and get to know many LEOs all over this country, and I'm proud to say they take the job very seriously. They are the ones who charge into the night, prepared to handle whatever gets thrown at them, and sometimes it's a lot to take. And they do it, without complaint, without regret, and without hesitation. Whether or not the community supports them in the moment, they do their best with what they've got, and I'll be damned if I'll turn my back on the ones who fight the good fight to keep people safe. I wish I could say that for all law enforcement, and maybe someday we will be able to. But for now I stand by the ones who do their job in the face of mounting pressure and stress because it's the *right thing to do*. I'm with them when they stand up against injustice, even if it pains them to do it against the very officers who have transgressed against the law they have sworn to uphold.

There are always going to be people who abuse power. As the saying goes, "Power corrupts, and absolute power corrupts absolutely." No truer words have ever been said. You see it all the time: someone finds themselves in a position where they have carte blanche control and people to satisfy their every whim, along with money and clout and everything else that comes with it. Whether it's corporate or political, it all comes out in the fucking laundry. Imelda Marcos, J. Edgar Hoover, Leona Helmsley, and, something tells me, the Cheeto too—all these people took their power to the extreme in the name of personal gain and ruthless control, lording over others with disgust and disdain. This is why our country was supposed to have checks and balances. This is why no one branch of the government should have more power than the other. This is why America must be careful when senators and representatives speak about "restructuring the branches of government"—that usually means someone's trying to pull something over on the American people.

But let's get back to what I agree with in the conservative pamphlet. The concept of smaller government has always been what they *say* they want, but all they're doing is moving the big spending and federal control around to other places on the Monopoly board. For every Democratic program that helps the arts and music in school, there's the Republicans waiting with a giant budget cut so they can funnel that money into national defense. For every Democratic welfare program that benefits the lower class, there's a Republican tax cut for the middle to upper class—not necessarily a bad thing but also not beneficial for the nation's budget. The new GOP hits the old talking points but really doesn't have any plans to drive costs down—as long as inflation is on their side, they can control the means of interest and profit until the cows come home. Smaller government, according to people like me who still appreciate the idea, means an even spread of federal and state legislation and lawmaking: all sides working as one, and no one side trying to filibuster or countermand ideas or laws. That's smaller government to me—the states have a handle on things and the federal level can augment but concentrate on things like foreign policy and overall oversight.

That, sadly, is not the case when you have so many states trying desperately to legislate horrible laws designed specifically to be prejudicial and biased. From the HB2 laws in North Carolina to the a-woman-is-just-a-host legislation introduced in Oklahoma to combat abortion, the states have gone off the deep end in a lot of unlawful ways, causing the Supreme Court to have to step in and rule against most of these ignorant, hateful attempts to oppress people and get us running backward into the decades where—*legally*—you could rape and beat your wife just after lynching a black man (depending on what state you were in). Thank goodness progress has slowed these advances toward ridiculous misanthropy. However, the specters of these kinds of foulness keep coming up every time we take the rugs out to beat the dust out of them. How can we trust the state governments to get on with business as usual when these same politicians are trying to spin the clocks back to a time when the only way to truly be a safe, law-abiding citizen was to be white?

It needs to start with voters in these states and counties getting together and *really* taking a look at what these cocksuckers are running on as far as their message. Now, most of the older generation is going to always vote with the party—nothing you can do about the obstinacies of the older generation. But the younger voters, the ones who question and worry about subtle things like, oh I don't know, *the future*, can do their research and see what kind of immoral message these dick brains are running on and help vote them the fuck out of office. These cannot be the days when we allow the party line to be just a bunch of party favors, serving no purpose but to distract from the line in the sand being crossed. This is where vigilance and concern will help stay the course and reverse the hate mongering disguised as cronyism that permeates so many candidates and so much reality. If we start at the foundation and *force* these politicians to really stand behind the statements and ideals of the communities at large, voting against the ones who are just trying to build a bigger better Tammany Hall, we *may* be able to lay the groundwork for that "smaller government" ideal like we always wanted. But it won't happen if we allow career politicians and lifer congressmen and women to maintain positions of government just to keep lining their fucking pockets with the greed of the Tweeds.

Obviously there's a handful of Republican stalwarts I don't agree with, like the anti-abortionists and welfare opponents. I make no qualms and give no fucks about being pro-choice all the way, regardless of being a father and family man myself. Also, having grown up on welfare, it's hard for me to argue against it, seeing as if it weren't for those subsidies, I wouldn't be alive today. Anti-abortion laws smack in the very face of the "small government" idea: you mean to tell me you're okay with gutting certain programs because it's not the government's job to handle it, but you'll reallocate funds to fight against abortion because you think it's the government's right to tell a *grown woman* what she can or can't do with her body? No wonder some of you motherfuckers look so god damn miserable: there's no *way* you're a hit with the ladies. Same goes for welfare: you'll gladly give all this money to the military even though we already have one of the largest and most technologically advanced armed forces on the planet, but you won't set aside just a little to help families in need? The hypocrisy of the right-wing agenda is hardly a well-kept secret, but sometimes I truly wonder if they hear themselves when they stick their own feet in their mouths and asses.

I've put my discussion of the Second Amendment toward the end because there is a *lot* to talk about, not least because it's one of the most important issues at stake but also because to me the answer is so simple, and yet so many people are so busy arguing about it that they refuse to see the truth of it. So I'll proceed with caution, but only up to a point. After all, it's something I'm passionate about as well, not only from a rights and freedoms standpoint but also from a "keep Americans safe" place as well.

To begin, I have met people affected by tragedies such as mass shootings and school massacres. I have known people who died because of the consequences of gun violence. Yet here I am, prepared to advocate for the Second Amendment because it is and always should be a strong piece of the bedrock of our foundation. The Second Amendment is not just some antiquated law designed to make simple folk feel empowered; it is one of the great things that keeps our country from being overrun, and I truly mean that. It is the ultimate check for the year-end balance. So please allow me to talk this out before you seize up and stop listening. This is about a compromise that guarantees a slight bit of gun control but also allows us to maintain our right to bear arms and to form a militia. So settle back and strap on your BIG BOY AND GIRL FANCY PANTS (I totally have mine on). Let's get into it.

First of all, how many of you actually *know* what the Second Amendment says? Any time any of this starts to come up, people start screaming about the government coming to take our guns or that anyone with a gun is a potential serial killer ready to shoot up school buses and all that bullshit rhetoric. This is because most people don't really understand what it says or means. So here's the actual text: "A well-regulated militia, being necessary to the security of a free state, the right of the people to keep and bear arms, shall not be infringed." That's it. That's the extent of the text on it. A lot of people seem to think there are several ways to interpret that, and I'm sure if you're actually trying to get away with some shady shit, you'd be right. However, if you're just looking at it from the original context, it's quite simple: we as Americans have the right to keep arms in case of threats to our freedoms, foreign or domestic. Honestly, that's *all* it means. Now I'm going to ask you a series of serious questions, and I want you to forget all those shitty platform buzzwords and catchphrases that organizations try to use against us. I want you to thoughtfully consider your answer, then truthfully say it out loud. Don't say what your dad or mom would say. Don't say what your husband or wife would say. Don't say what your family always says, what your friends say, what your local boosters say, or anything like that. I want to know how you *really* want to answer.

First question: Does anything in that text make you feel like you need automatic weapons to hunt here in the United States? Hmm? Anything? I swear to god, if anyone tries to bring up bear attacks or some shit like that, I will crack like a window in a Dario Argento movie. Nothing in that fucking text gives any American the right to hunt deer with AR-15s or .50-caliber mini-guns or anything like that. If you seriously need those guns to *hunt*, you're a pussy who can't shoot. Sorry, my opinion. Second question: Does anything in that text make you feel like you need an arsenal equipped with more weapons than you have people in your house? Let me explain before you answer. I can understand and support a large family household that has multiple weapons because that makes sense: each person would have their own gun. It doesn't mean they're a bunch of fucking doomsday preppers stocking up for the Purge; it just means that, according to the Constitution, they are legally armed and prepared in case we're invaded or a despot goes crazy and decides he's going to sic the military on us or law enforcement goes rogue and we need to defend ourselves. In our country that may seem like a crazy idea, but it's *because* of the fact that it happens in other countries that we've made sure we are equipped to handle the situation. It does *not* mean a weirdo living in his mom's basement needs enough guns and explosives to recreate one of the "wolverines" scenes in *Red Dawn*. I don't give a fuck if that offends you pricks who have a shit-ton of weapons for no good reason other than to be obnoxious—fuck you. You're part of the problem.

I'll tell you exactly why you're part of the fucking problem: there are so many guns just lying around, unchecked or unrecorded, that random guns are getting into the wrong hands, and it's just one more way that tragedies from gun violence or school massacres happen. I'm certainly not saying it's the *only* reason, so just stop that fucking stupid thought from coming out of your dumb mouth. I *am* saying it's a reason. Just as it's incredibly easy to get a gun in various ways, it's also easy for a gun to go missing under someone's nose if they have so many that they can't keep track of them. If you're a single asshole in a one-bedroom apartment, you don't need to be able to re-arm Fort Bragg, for fuck's sake. Get over yourself and your delusional sense that you're entitled to roll like Arnold in *Commando*. We have the right to defend ourselves against fascism; we do not have the right to just stockpile and then cry like little bitches when people get upset about gun violence. Guess what? Guns cause violence. These motherfuckers who try to label guns as tools can suck it. When was the last time you built a house with a .357? When was the last time you used a .45 to gauge what the weather was going to be like? How's Google running on your fucking Uzi? Kiss my entire ass with that shit, or miss me with it, whichever keeps your fucking breath from turning shitty.

And before some of you liberals start cranking up your hype machine, slow your damn roll. I do have another side to this argument. Trying to push through too much gun control is unconstitutional, and you know it. I have every sympathy for parents, friends, and family affected by gun violence. I do. I've lost people to this sort of violence myself—more than you'll know. But it has not changed my mind in the slightest about how I feel about our right to bear arms because that's not about the guns; it's about the mental health issues in our country or the lack of any threat of retribution in lieu of the consequences of your actions, like I talked about before. Now I know it's a little harder for me to talk about, seeing as the federal government has tried to deregulate the legislation that prohibits anyone with mental health issues from having a gun legally. Even I can't understand the fucking thought process behind that. But this isn't about the guns themselves; like it or not, we are an armed nation. It makes Americans cautious on the streets, but it also keeps certain international powers at bay if the thought of a North American invasion ever crosses their scheming little minds. It's a double-edged sword; we cannot keep overreacting every time something happens. The moderation inherent in our systems needs to come to the surface and help us all get on the same page, and that goes for *both* sides of the coin. Responsible gun owners who deplore the tragedies need to speak up, above the NRA and all the other organizations only interested in making fucking money, not guaranteeing your rights as a citizen. On the other side, responsible progressives need to step up and understand that one gunman does not represent the whole of gun owners and should look to solve the individual situations, not design some shit catchall that ostracizes law-abiding Americans in its legal nets. I know more people who are responsible with guns than I do people who are morons with them, so I can safely say a new dialogue needs to open, and soon.

Can't we all just get along?

Circling back to smaller government, this is one of the reasons I think Americans should talk more to *each other* than let the politicians do the talking for us. The politicians hand down a bunch of old, busted scripts they intend to be parroted around like commercials on repeat. They do it often enough that most of us start thinking that shit's the truth. It's not the truth—it's control. They design these crazy things to get us all fired up and screaming, going for each other's throats because we can't get to the ones who freaked us out in the first place: the assholes in office. Guess what, Solomon? Some of us are onto your shtick, and we're letting others know the secret to your shell game. Most people *don't* want violence, riots, or pain for anyone; they just want to live their lives knowing that business is being handled, their money is being managed properly, and that those who are in charge aren't running around like Nero setting fires and singing about it. Quite frankly, that's not a tall order to hope for in a country that pleads poverty yet breeds billionaires. What it boils down to is peace of mind for good eggs, to healing, not concealing the pain. The future isn't just yours or mine—it belongs to everyone.

Any real conservative with a head on his shoulders can't support Trump unless they're just running it down the line. Donald

Trump: a man who declares bankruptcy like a person declares what they'll have to eat at a fast-food restaurant. Donald Trump: a man who's terrified to show people his taxes or live in the White House. Donald Trump: a man who is trying to cut all kinds of spending but isn't bothered by the burden on the American taxpayer that comes from security and whatnot around Trump Tower in New York City. Donald Trump: a man who talks real tough but lies and lies and lies and lies and lies and fucking lies. Fuck the fascist Cheeto. He does *not* speak for the working man. He does *not* represent the lower or middle classes. He does *not* know what it takes to live a normal life out in the fucking world today. He screams about tightening belts while he poses for photos in his rooms gilded with gold. What he *means* is "everyone else is going to have to tighten their fucking belts so they can pay for my lifestyle in office." He's a fucking insult to real men and women who bust their ass for a living. You can say whatever you want about me and come at me with "what do you know about being poor if you're rich?" I'll tell you right now: I am not rich. I am young enough to remember what it was like to be hungry and poor and scared to death. I am old enough to fight and scrape and work to make sure my family doesn't ever feel the shit that I went through. What do I know? More than that piece-of-shit president.

Men like Trump are an insult to my uncle Jim and others like him. They use loopholes like other people use entries and exits. There's a lot I agree with on the Republican platform, but there's a lot I will *never* support or agree with, nor will I ever understand why decent, hard-working people would support it with a figurehead like the Cheeto out in front, like some deranged master of ceremonies, lying about wiretaps and terrorists and Russia and all kinds of other shit that never fucking goes anywhere.

Usually normal folks can smell a con artist a mile away. This one? Well, fuck, they voted for him. It'll all come out in the wash soon enough. When it does, it's going to sting, and a lot of people are going to lash out and fuck with each other because we're all human and that's what we do. But I'll tell you what else we do: we get over it and on with it. The blood and muscle of this country comes not from these pricks on their high horses or pedestals but from the middle, the center and the heart of America. We are not the poor. We are not the rich. We are right down the line. We represent millions of people who fought to get a little closer to the golden ticket. Sometimes we get both hands on it and cash it in. Sometimes all we get is a vanilla wafer. But being here in this country, very rarely are we disappointed. It's part of the power of the dream. Most modern GOP members think it only belongs to people a shade lighter than pieces of notebook paper. That's why they don't deserve to claim the rights to the American dream: they don't know that Americans look like everyone, not just themselves.

I know I'm a misogynistic, white American male who loves guns and women. I know that when it all comes down to it, I have no real right to speak for any member of any minority, or the opposite sex, or a different sexual orientation. I know that experience speaks louder than wishes when it comes to how we should all treat each other. I also know that sort of smacks in the face of the Republican base—or at least that's what they'd have you believe. When all is said and done, many of us might see things differently. That doesn't mean we need to give up how we feel politically, but it might mean we could take a step toward understanding what we *all* need, not just what they tell us *we* need: *only* us. Come to think of it, we might think about looking at other people's needs a little more often. Republican politicians will tell you that's a hard-core liberal Democrat thing to do. No, it's not a liberal thing to do; it's a *human* thing to do. If the GOP wants to hold onto good people in their foundation, they need to realize this before it's too late. Someday the time will come when they might throw open their doors to let in some light and offer people a seat at the table so they can push their conservative agenda. If they don't realize that an agenda that never allows help for people in need is anathema to being alive in general, those doors won't be darkened by anyone with good standing ever again.

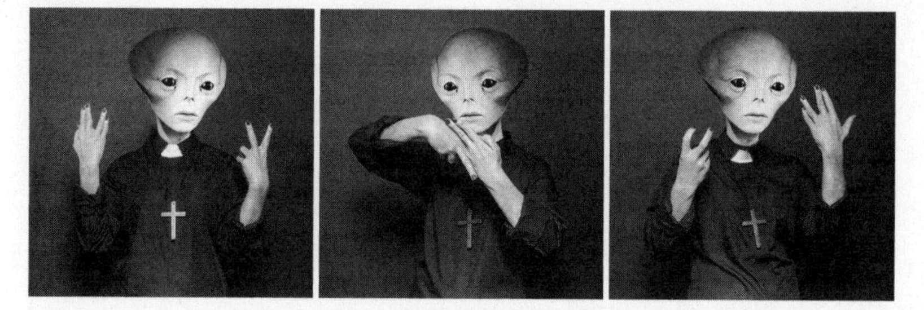

CHAPTER 10

MOTHER, JUGS, SPEED, SACCO, AND VANZETTI

HAVE YOU EVER HEARD OF WORD OF MOUTH?

Well, fucking duh, of course you have.

It's not quite legend, it's not quite rumor, but it's elements of both, twisted with hints of truth, fact, and fancy. Word of mouth is akin to "word on the street," the "buzz," what all the hubbub's about, after all. Word of mouth spreads like fire on a gasoline lake, seeking dark corners and light conversation to burn, burn, burn with life. It gets caught up in fervor and makes people crazy with anticipation, hope, and desire, ready to fan the flames across a generation. Word of mouth has built kingdoms, toppled governments, fueled the zeitgeist, and cemented the histories of a million different overnight sensations. Word of mouth can be good—or bad—for the soul. Yes, it creates a vision of possibility, but it can also make it impossible to exceed expectations. Beware the pretty people selling beautiful miracles: just when you think you can afford it, the interest rates go through the roof and down through the floorboards.

Word of mouth gave us Guns N' Roses, Nirvana, and, for the most part, a certain metal band from Iowa. Word of mouth turned us on to fads like Candy Crush and Words with Friends. It led us to ditch MySpace for the greener pastures of Facebook, then to the magnificent minimalism of Twitter, then Instagram, then Snapchat, and so on and so forth. Word of mouth makes mountains out of icons and molehills out of the past tense. It can perpetuate a gorgeous lie if the pop is loud enough and kill the better brand if its sex tape doesn't make you harder or wetter right fucking *now*. Word of mouth is something you can't buy. Awesome word of mouth is Barack Obama. Shitty word of mouth is Donald Drumpf.

These United States of America and the singular body it goes by have always had fantastic word of mouth. Everywhere you go on this planet, you tend to hear the same thing: "In America you can *do* anything, *go* anywhere, and *be* anyone. In America FREEDOM IS REAL." Well, at least they *used* to say that. That was before "the deplorables" started building walls and closing borders all because they are terrified of brown people. (Please put on your Big-Person Grownup Sarcasm Goggles again, folks.) And why shouldn't they be? We *all* know that brown people are the biggest threat to the planet, our country, our children, and our monies! Brown people attack us for no reason, shit on our credit lines with no thought of our well-being, and are hell bent on setting fire to our gods! They took d'ey gods! What are we supposed to do as they take d'ey gods?! This is 'MURICA! We need d'ey gods! (You may now take off your Big Person Grownup Sarcasm Goggles. But you should still keep them close.)

So, to backtrack, I'm not sure too many people are singing our praises lately. But for all intents and purposes it does still ring true, especially to those who never set foot on our fruited plains, our homes of the brave. Coming here from somewhere like Syria, North Korea, or any of the other fascist/communist/combat zones, this country of ours is a fucking Shangri-La; the sun shines, the waters are clear, and you can run as far and as fast as you care to in America. At least that's what all the ads say. That's the message all the commercials beat you over the head with, anyway. I'm not here to dissuade people that this isn't true—far from it. I hope to reinforce it. However, there's an America no one talks about, an America that only really gets coverage on the night-and-day news channels. This is where the fine print gets the magnifying glass.

Our word of mouth, nine times out of ten, can be a lie.

We're only "free" if we're whiter than most. We're only "richer" than our neighbors if we're that alabaster-skinned type. We're only "safe" if we're in the right neighborhoods, on the right streets, with the right people—sure, the whiter people. I don't give a shit if that stings some white people. Not *all* white people think that way, but it's true. Because of this, white people have a certain idea of what this country *ought* to be. It ought not have so many refugees or immigrants, illegal or otherwise. It ought to have a level of control on criminals, but *not* our guns. It ought to know exactly what its *real* citizens need. This snowy-white bullshit is exactly why there is *so much* resentment against people of my pale complexion. No matter what I do to counterbalance it, the entitlement and privilege undoes so much good that it's no wonder that as of this writing in 2017, we are closer to civil war than we've been in 150 years. It's sickening to me how my fellow Americans are treated because of what color they are, all because white Americans can't be bothered to retrain themselves about what this country *really stands for*.

Don't get me wrong: I love my country. I would fight and die for my country, and I still believe in my country. However, before my country can change, it needs to embrace its own chaos factor. The United States could get a lot out of an AA twelve-step program, meaning the first step toward fixing a problem is acknowledging you *have* a problem in the first place. Until you do so, this country will continue walking in the wind, trapped in a box with no escape. This will not be easy, I'm afraid: America is as complicated as its foreign policies. It has layers upon layers of intricate subsections that blur lines between good and bad, real and fake, screams and whispers and songs of our past. I love this country with all my heart, but there is nothing I hate worse than the way *we* as Americans treat each other, stepping on each other's rights and repeating the horrible shit that others spew into the atmosphere like mustard gas on a Belgian battlefield. We're eating each other—why? Because self-importance tastes like cotton candy in our country.

Speaking of being white, I have a terrible habit of forgetting that I *am* white. Now there are several ways you can look at that. You can say, "Oh, look at the shitty hippy who doesn't 'see color.' He's so edgy because he doesn't see himself as white." You can also say, "Oh, check out the privilege coming off Captain Dick over here. Only a white person could get away with forgetting their color." Both are valid, vicious, and good satirical points, to be taken seriously for the most part. I really wish it were something slightly profound like that, if not also a tad on the abrasive side. No, no, regrettably, it is far more ridiculous than those examples. It really comes down to the fact that I get very distracted in my own head with my own shit and forget what color I am. Now, granted, I will admit there are very few moments when my color comes into question, unlike my other multicolored brothers and sisters. I think this is where America has its biggest problem: no one can agree on what an American looks like. If you ask any American what a citizen looks like, they'll describe someone who looks very much like they do. Fair enough: we all identify with people who are more like ourselves. The issue comes around when you ask them what an American does *not* look like. The answers will not surprise you or make you feel proud. We talked about that earlier, and it's not a specifically American idea of lily-pale nationalism, but the volume does tend to get cranked up on it. This is, of course, the USA we're talking about: everything we do goes to eleven.

Yes, I forget I'm white sometimes because I don't really give a shit, to be honest. I've never understood people who are proud of being white. Black Pride, Brown and Proud, Asian Love—I understand all those ideas. It's about celebrating your heritage and history in the face of pain and adversity. It's about never forgetting what your people have done, no matter who's keeping score and writing it down. White people don't need that—we've been the ones writing and rewriting history since we wrested the pens from the historians' hands. So White Pride has never made sense to me. Then again, I have other interests. Most people who are obsessed with White Pride are usually not very good at anything else. Surely they're convinced that they're good at being white, but can that happen? Can you be good at being a color? These people seem to believe so. But from where I'm standing, it kind of looks like they're shitty at it. White people are no better than anyone else. There are a lot of Trumpy snowflakes who will take umbrage with that statement, but it doesn't make it any less true. Why would there be anything awesome about being white? We've never had to fight for attention or acceptance—*ever*. We usually take up civil disobedience as a hobby; other ethnicities have dedicated their *lives* to fighting for equality because if they don't fight for it, nothing *ever* gets done. Sometimes even when it *does* get done, you never know when it'll be undone in another person's lifetime by some asshole with a pinch more power. White people? Most are part time, like Uber.

I can see why white people try to identify being American almost exclusively as white, because the two concepts have a lot in common: being white and being American are largely linked because they can both take an idea, blow it out of proportion, and *choose* to play the victim or the hero. Americans *love* the role of drama queen, complete with Maybelline, marijuana, and martyrdom. Americans are always ready to protest or celebrate. This goes back to what we talked about earlier: when everything is offensive, nothing is offensive. When everything causes outrage, nothing will cause outrage. Americans are very good at getting whipped up into a frenzy, whether it's warranted or not. Sure, during the Cheeto's first ten days in office he gave us several reasons to be pissed off. Even those who voted for him were starting to get that burn in their belly. Meanwhile, Trump supporters were threatening a boycott of Starbucks—*again*—because the CEO had vowed to hire refugees (internationally, by the way, not *just* in America) in response to Trump's immigration ban. Trumpers were outraged because it "took jobs away from Americans." People, listen: if Starbucks was going to be a viable job choice for you, you would have applied there by now. There's that white privilege shining through again: it's hard to bitch about unemployment when you tend to have the benefit of being choosy.

But you can't talk like that about America to certain people. It's another reason we're in such vast fuckery right now. When you can't have a conversation with your fellow country folk, whether conciliatory or accusatory, without a screaming match breaking out, bordering on fisticuffs, you're standing on a cultural fault line, just waiting for the earth to crack and swallow us alive.

Guess what: there's shit about this country that fucking sucks. Sorry. Historically our track record for equality has, ironically, not been the best. Economically we seem to prefer extremes to the center that needs attention. Some would rather rape our natural resources than keep our country's landscapes intact. We are not colorblind, even keeled, morally superior, overly exceptional, bulletproof, extraordinary, or untouchable. It's been a while since we've had our ass kicked. I'm not talking about a national tragedy like 9/11 or Pearl Harbor; I would never wish that on us or anyone else. Maybe this whole Trump thing is exactly what we needed: to realign our beliefs again and remind us that our diversity is an asset, not a deficit.

Nietzsche said, "God is dead." But don't tell other Americans that.

You have to realize that most Americans refuse to think that anything is correct outside of what they hear on Fox News or MSNBC. Most Americans just want to get on with it and kick out the jams. They *love* gawd, booze, man buns, muscle cars and Priuses, being rednecks and millennials, PBR, meth, strawberry meth . . . and tons of guns to go with it all. In other words, Americans love being perpetual dick-lickers, in any guise that particular brand of licker happens to take. Americans know how to have a good time, even in the face of a crazy global catastrophe. That's why people go to such great lengths to have the cleverest sign at the protest. That's why they need to have the most offensive T-shirt at the rally. We as Americans aren't moderate about anything—hell, we even take moderation to extremes. It's fucking ridiculous, hilarious, and secretly terrifying. It's never enough to make a point—we always need to make a statement. It's never enough to make sense—we need to make you *agree* with us at all fucking costs. If you deviate from our agreement, you're a no-good, sniveling, commie cocksucker or you're a bigoted, bullying Nazi. I use both choices because I just described both sides of the burning bed.

I don't have time for rhetoric. I only have time for reruns of *Scooby-Doo*.

I was visiting a family member in the hospital not long after the election. The staff was getting her room ready for her, so I was standing in the waiting area with some others from my family. There were other families in there waiting as well, and someone had put on Fox News. Now, I am not a huge fan of watching the news outside my home—I also have a hard time with these channels being on in every airport, everywhere you look—but I was not the one to put it on, so I did my best to mind my own business. It was going well until one of the dads connected to a different family took a phone call and began to go on a diatribe over Fox News. "Yeah, I'm here! Yep, he's going to be sworn in, then he's going to PUT THE BITCH IN JAIL!" This last retort made me look up from my phone. He was staring into the TV with unhidden glee, smiling from ear to ear. "It's about time somebody did something about her! She's a goddamn criminal and she deserves to be LOCKED UP!" Now, you didn't have to be a Rhodes Scholar to figure out who he was talking about. I'd heard enough hoopla and horse shit during the election and debates to know that every zealot with a red baseball cap thought Hillary Clinton was a criminal for nothing more than some emails on a server—something, by the way, other men before had done as well, but nobody really wanted to talk about that.

I was standing there, listening to this man go on and on to the unseen listener about the evils of HRC, when I noticed his teenage kids. They were miserable. There was a boy and a girl, and they looked like they were doing their very best to not only become one with the chair they were sitting in but also to fold themselves into tinier pieces for tucking into the cushions. I knew that look: they'd sat through this same tirade night after night, day after day, for months, maybe even a fucking year, and they were appalled it was happening again, yet this time in a public place, with other ears present for listening, which you could easily do because he was bellowing like a doomsayer on his coffee break. I looked at his kids, then back at him, and then back at his kids again, then I got up, slowly went over to the table in the middle of the room where the remote control sat, picked it up, and turned it to the USA Network. I'm not sure if it was merely the look of embedded dread on his children's face that changed my mind or if it was the edgy look of hateful frost commingling with heady triumph on his face. But I'd simply had enough. It'd be one thing if he were in his own home—none of my business there. But he wasn't the only one in the room, and I wasn't going to listen to it.

The second the channel changed, he snapped out of it angrily, like a smoker looking for his lost lighter. He looked up and over at me with an accusatory expression that said, *What are you doing, and who the hell do you think you are?* I didn't care. I didn't even say anything. I just let him watch me scan the room, let him take in the fact that there were other people around who didn't need to listen to his bullshit. Then I let my gaze rest on his kids, who were only then coming out from under their jackets and shirts, checking to see if the air was still clean to breathe. When he took notice of his children's reaction, he paused as if he knew he was in the wrong. Then some sort of righteous indignation caught him by the collar, and he gave me a shitty look of contempt. I didn't even flinch: I've seen that look before, and it no longer bothers me. So I let him waste his energy on trying to get on my nerves. Finally he just got up and stormed out. I gave the remote to my aunt, who was sitting nearest the television. When my head came up I suddenly noticed for the first time that his children had directed their attention toward me. We all stared for a second, then they smiled briefly. I gave them a smirk and a quick shrug, then went to check on our "patient." I never suffer fools lightly, but when I see that their families are suffering as well, I tend to get very, very aggressive.

I'll be honest, and you can laugh at the irony and hypocrisy later: I hate talking politics anymore. It is fucking exhausting. There's nothing worse than getting into a real-life flame war with some twat who thinks he's the intellectual equivalent of Salmon P. Chase, trying desperately to get you as fired up as he is. Worse yet is the "Google-ist": someone who is just ready and waiting for you to say something that they can refute by using Google to pull a bunch of facts and figures out of their gaping, goochless assholes. "I *hate* to disagree with you Corey"—which is code for "I've been dying to disagree with you Corey"—"but putting your trust in the mainstream media is pointless when you take into account that 90 percent of the media is *owned* by six corporations." Yeah, that's great and all, but I'm not a fucking moron: I tend to do a *bit* of research before I believe anything I hear. I don't take one media outlet as gospel; I check all the networks, newsfeeds, and databases before I come to my conclusions. Sure, some of the news channels are owned by the same companies, but not *all* of them are. So anyone who doesn't give me the benefit of the doubt doesn't get invited back to the Tuesday Boiled-Egg Bruncheon, which is kind of a big deal on my block, just saying . . .

I'd also be shocked if anyone knew who Salmon P. Chase was, outside of Ohio, without Googling him for confirmation.

It's a weird world we live in. More people believe in angels than in aliens, a good percentage still do not believe that we walked on the moon yet wholeheartedly believe in the existence of Bigfoot, and almost all are pasted to their couches any time a Kardashian comes on TV because they believe that family is just the epitome of grace and style. Do you *see* how deluded we've become? The "fake news" thing that the New Nazis are using to breed distrust has done them well—a lot of people have no fucking clue what's going on anymore, and when they do, they're just parroting what the White House pulled from Breitbart that day. The propaganda wing of the Trump administration is We, The People—well, *you*, the people. I don't believe a red cent, a white lie, or a blue fuck that comes out of that entire fucking government's mouths. You must understand that I'm not pulling for one side or the other—I HONESTLY THINK YOU ARE ALL FUCKED IN THE FUCKING HEADS. I have a sneaking suspicion that if there were ever a time when you all thought no one was looking, you'd eat your young and go after the infirm next. I don't have very nice things to think about any one of you. I'm pretty sure you feel the same way about me. *So what's the difference?* you may ask. It's really simple: ask me if I give a shit what you think.

I have a very vivid memory of a moment right out of a Bruce Springsteen video—in fact, in this memory the Boss was playing on the radio. I could hear it on our neighbor's radio in their Bronco: "My Hometown." It was his latest single at the time, which tells you how long ago it was. Anyway, this memory is straight from the heart of the American ideal. The sun was shining down, hot and bright, onto white houses and green grass. There was just enough breeze to take the edge off the heat. None of the backyards had any fence; all the lawns ran together to make one long maze of lush paths and sober living. A few clotheslines swayed with the wind, and in the gravel driveways of a couple of the homes grown men were bent under the hoods of their cars, furiously toiling at the engines, oil filters, transmissions, and so on and so forth. It was quiet save for that Springsteen song, wavy and unfiltered, carrying across the static like pine needles scraping out a tune on solid vinyl. Other than the music, the scene was gravely still. This was the score to a ghost town. This was a siesta in Tombstone. All around me were the real American colors: blue, black, yellow, green, white, gray, and dabs of red and purple here and there, but Bob Ross wouldn't have needed much blending if he'd been bent at his easel trying to capture this moment. This was simply a blip on the map. This was a space between the American heartbeats.

I remember this moment not because of anything in particular but because of how it looked. I was probably thirteen years old, right around the time of my Semi Trip (just wait until the next chapter). In that moment I found myself hyper-aware of everything that was making that scene so vivid for me. This was the fabled American Dream. This was apple pie and freedom and eagles shooting lasers out of T-shirt cannons. This was Lincoln and Washington bare-knuckle boxing for the souls of their troops. This was the Promised Land, full of all the things anyone could ever want: peace, quiet, love, honor, chocolate, and cold Bud on tap. It was a Norman Rockwell wet dream, complete with children nursing ice cream headaches and dogs looking for a hydrant to use so the grass didn't lose its color. Oh, it was a regular Shangri-La just off Main Street, USA.

Of course, it was all a lie.

Yeah man, are you fucking kidding me? Everyone in that neighborhood dealt crank when they weren't beating their spouses. The kids were dicks, the dogs were rabid, the air smelled like weed and exhaust, all the cars were up on blocks because they didn't run (didn't really matter if the engines worked or not—none of them had wheels anyway), and the grass was interrupted on all sides by the junkyards that bordered that little hamlet. It was pure folly: Fool's Gold Paradise. I knew it then and I know it now—there is *no* singular view of the United States of America. Every city, town, state, county, coast, quarter, section, region, area, and arena is completely different, and though we all have stunning similarities regardless of distance, those differences are one of the reasons we represent one of the most fascinating countries on Planet Earth. From the Mason-Dixon Line to the Continental Divide, the good ol' US-of-A is so diverse in its scenery, cultures, peoples, landscapes, seasons, and raison d'êtres that you could try to cover it with as many pictures and examples as possible, and you'd never scratch the surface. Its faces are as varied as its languages; its scars as deep as any ocean and as painful as any tragedy. So when the White House, in its *infinite* wisdom, writes a statement on National Holocaust Remembrance Day—a day *specifically* about the Holocaust of World War II—and that statement makes no mention about the atrocities committed against the Jews, instead choosing to make some half-assed poke about "they weren't the only ones affected by the Holocaust," that sends a clear message to people who aren't fucking stupid: CERTAIN AMERICANS ARE BETTER THAN OTHERS, CERTAIN PEOPLE ARE BETTER THAN OTHERS, AND CERTAIN LIVES MATTER MORE THAN MOST. It's disgusting on a level that most white people can't fathom. Why? Because they have no real understanding of a pain or a violation like that.

Forgive me, but I'm going to get *really* fucking serious on you all right now.

All I hear from people all the fucking time is, "You have to give Trump a chance." This is the mantra I keep hearing from my friends who are conservative across the board, not just fiscally like myself. They keep nudging me and saying, "Okay, it looks bad, but you *have* to give Trump a *chance*." I thought about it. Really, I did. For a few weeks I just sat and observed, trying to wrestle my anger back into its restraints and log chains. I did my very best to put aside my vitriol on the great Cheeto and waited to give him a chance. So I watched—watched as he nominated shithead after shithead to this cabinet, including a woman auspiciously for Secretary of Education who not only pushes a very faith-based lesson program heavy on Creationism but also misspelled several words on Inauguration Day. I watched as the Cheeto kept getting bent out of shape like a petulant cunt, going on his late-night Twitter rants, accusing CNN of being fake news (Christ, he even managed to work it into his statement for Black History Month) and *Saturday Night Live* and the *New York Times* of being irrelevant. I watched as his cabinet tried desperately to push through an immigration ban that would protect *no one* yet discriminate against millions of *specific* people. I watched as the Cheeto blew up on North Korea, Iran, Mexico, Australia . . . and yet not one fucking word about Russia. I watched as millions of people, for better or worse, marched in nearly every city around the world in solidarity against this president. I'd never seen anything like it. I've lived through eight other POTUSes, and I have never seen this level of revilement in my entire life. But still, people are asking me to give him a chance. He has a fucking white nationalist press boy who looks like he showers in dumpster juice and a vice president who could be a stunt double for Ed Harris on *Westworld*. But I should give him a chance. No one has seen his wife since the inauguration, but people continue to call his *daughter* the First Lady. But I should give him a chance. He and his cabinet are causing Americans to tear this country apart. But I should give him a chance.

I don't think so.

His ego refuses to admit that there's anything wrong with what's being said and done in his name or with his terrible version of "leading." His narcissism won't allow him to have an apologetic side, making him push his shitty chips in on a bet that no one can win. He is in a constant state of resting cunt face, physically incapable of distinguishing between falling asleep while angry and painfully explosive diarrhea. He gives off the impression of a joyless, bloodless, calculating cocksucker with no regard for anyone's well-being other than his own—not even his children or his wife. These qualities might actually be effective in a leader if they didn't look like they swallowed tiny children the way boa constrictors do. He's too odd looking to be a Bond villain and too severe to be taken lightly. He has surrounded himself with yes men and women to keep his id on stroke. There are signals and there are warnings. So before I go any fucking further and give myself an aneurysm with this level of stupidity, tell me again why I should give him a fucking chance. Even if I took into consideration what might be a few good ideas for our financial futures, he's still *not* a good leader. He's *not*. I will gladly debate this until the day I fucking die. The Cheeto is *not* a good leader. I mean, who the *fuck* starts shit with Australia?!

I'm no kumbaya hippy-dippy dipshit. I don't expect people to get along, hold hands, hug, and make out all the time while they make Robitussin brownies and read Archie Zombie comics. I have no illusions about how evolved we *actually* are. I know we still have a need for capital punishment and our Second Amendment rights. I know people tend to get monster hard-ons for each other, causing them to assault with extreme prejudice. But I *do* expect our leader to keep his fucking cool. I do expect him (or her) to at least *try* to bring us all together instead of merely strengthen his fucking base. I expect him to at least *try* to pretend to give a shit about other people. You can't do that when you specifically narrow the scope of the internal terrorism laws to be more Islam-centric and to let Neo-Nazis off the fucking hook. You don't do that by making it painfully clear that the whiter you are, the better off you'll be in Trump's America.

In *my* America people embrace each other like a good bag of M&Ms—you know what you got is awesome on the inside, whether or not the outside is different. We've been given this gift of a country, and yet none of us can figure out who deserves to be here. Well, I *say* "given," even though we *did* kind of help ourselves to this land, taking advantage of a culture that had no system of ownership or money. Then we kicked them all across the country after telling them, "Okay, *this* time, we *swear* we won't take this land from you! You guys can *totally* have this to live on without any of us screaming 'imminent domain' on you again! *Look*—no crossed fingers or eyes or toes! It's all yours!" Anyone who doesn't have family in the various native tribes of this land is a refugee and an immigrant. Our ancestors either came here to escape or were brought here. So seeing as this country was *founded* by refugees and immigrants, let me give you a little taste of who looks and feels like an American.

America looks like Samuel, the fifty-four-year-old black American pastor who gets up early every morning to take his grandchildren to school, then goes to his church to look after his congregation. It looks like Maya, the Muslim American making a living as a waitress while she works her way through college. It looks like Rosa, a Latin American doing everything she can to keep her family together because some were born here and some were born in Mexico. It looks like Brian, a Caucasian American who works with his brothers at their father's mill when he's not serving with the National Guard on the weekends. It looks like Jim, an Asian American who works with teenagers to keep them out of gangs and with their families instead of homeless and addicted to drugs. It looks like all these people, all their families, all their friends, all their *friends'* families, and everyone else I haven't even thought of. This is America, not that vanilla, boring, bullshit, "whites only" version that some of these fanatics would love to have. Besides, if they get rid of all the black people, Hispanic people, Asians, Muslims, Jews, members of the native tribes, and any color other than "notebook paper," who the fuck will they all find to hate? Huh? The easy answer is each other, but that's a little *too* easy, right? Wouldn't it be funny to see Klansmen, all confused and full of shitty hate, burning crosses in front of rabbit holes or doghouses? How weird would it be watching these racist mooks trying to keep different breeds of cats or birds from hanging out together? The pure state of frustration in their tiny little minds would hopefully cause cerebral hemorrhaging. But the crazy part of this whole idea is that it's *their* country too. No matter how upset we get, no matter how out of whack their ideas about people of color are, this is America. If they're not advocating harming another person, they can say and think whatever they want.

That's right: the First Amendment of the Bill of Rights protects any type of speech that is not deemed "hate speech" and doesn't advocate violence. This is one of the bedrocks this country was built upon—and you're not going to like this, but there's absolutely nothing wrong with that. Before you egg my house, TP my trees, and soap my fucking windows, HEAR ME THE FUCK OUT. I'm not advocating for what the Klan, the Westboro Baptist Church, or any of the other hate groups say; I am against everything they stand for. And I know that they *do* tend to advocate for violence against anyone who can't blend in with a bed sheet. But if they're not calling for action against the other races, it's protected by the Constitution of the United States. I'm sorry, but it is. This is why I get so fucking upset about the crazy angry violent protests against Milo Yiannopoulos's speaking engagements. Do you realize that by starting riots and setting fires at his events (and any other place you're not happy about, honestly) you are no fucking better than they are? By answering their cries for mediocre fascism with the same viciousness and anger, you have become the fucking problem yourselves. Same thing with all the protests against the Cheeto: all you are doing is galvanizing his base and steeling them against any common sense you might be making. You're basically guaranteeing his re-election. So pick your fucking spots, and as for the rest, KNOCK IT THE FUCK OFF, YA PANSY-ASS COCKSUCKERS.

This shit is *not* rocket science. It's not even fucking science. It's machinery. We all need each other for this country to run smoothly. The business folks need the landscaping folks. The artist folks need the trucking folks. The music folks need the travel folks (and the trucking folks). Every collar in America, from white to blue, needs each other. Every class in the United States must rely on each other, no exceptions. We are the bacteria that keeps this living organism with a red-white-and-blue flag running and chugging along. We all need to coalesce, coexist, and understand one thing: WE ARE NOT ALL GOING TO FUCKING GET ALONG, BUT THAT DOES NOT MEAN WE ARE GOING TO FIGHT CONSTANTLY. Sorry, hippies. We are not evolved enough to appreciate each other for our souls yet, so we're going to have to get by on tolerating for the sake of peace. There's nothing wrong with that sentiment when you take into consideration that even if we were all fucking sedated and faded and free, we'd still be finding shit to hate on when no one's looking. Utopia doesn't exist; there's no such thing as the world commune. I'm not saying that it *can't* happen. I'm not even saying I wouldn't like to see that shit happen. I'd *love* to shed cloth and go around shirtless in sweatpants because looks and color and culture don't matter. But I'm also a pragmatist. The world we know is fractious and ragged, beaten down by centuries of programming telling us that anyone different is suspicious and, therefore, the enemy. This mentality is boiled down to one sentiment: "If you're not like me, I don't like you." We need to completely re-evaluate not only how we approach each other but also how we look at ourselves. If we immediately assume a stranger is inferior, we will always enter every conversation saturated with contempt and condescension.

We are a society made up of saints, thieves, killers, critics, lovers, builders, artists, and businessmen. We are the parts that make the sum "something else, indeed." We are the country that has broken every promise we've made to every race, religion, republic, and rebellion in our nearly 250 years of existence. We have saved some, invaded others, and sold the rest down the river of deceit. History may look on us with a sense of sad purpose, but for now we're outpacing our bad publicity as fast as we can. In this reality, in this universe, our word of mouth is still holding strong, beckoning the tired, the hungry, and those huddled masses of yesteryear, pushing hair out of dirty faces and gently telling the gypsy spirits that everything will be okay, you're here now, and "here" means the land of the free, the home of the brave, and a partridge in a pear tree. The world is onto us now; it knows we're not perfect. But as long as idealists like myself keep the faith and the fire burning, maybe that word of mouth won't have that shade of satire to it, that sense of two-faced debauchery. Maybe it'll hold up in court if enough of us testify. Nevertheless, there's a reason we're the bogeymen in a lot of countries regardless of what the politics are, the devil-headed democracy bent on owning the world—not even ruling it but *owning* it, because "Master makes money on the rent, not the upkeep."

So do me a fucking favor. Everybody listening out there? You in the back, digging in your ear, pay attention. We all know you're going to forget you were digging in your ear, then stick your finger in your mouth and make yourself throw up on the taste of earwax. So listen up.

If you've got some petty shit holding you back from really acknowledging and familiarizing yourself with your neighbors or other people in general, remind yourself of this little nugget, like a super-tight snap on the waistband of your brain: everything you find offensive that makes you hate in a stereotypical way, remember you can find all that same shit in people of your own color, your own creed, and your own sexuality. America is black, brown, red, yellow, white, gay, straight, and free to be so. Oh and by the way, if it isn't hurting anyone, it's also none of my or your fucking business. I'm not trying to create contention; I'm trying to expand the way people look at each other. If we *know* we're different and we don't *expect* each other to be the same, maybe we'll get over ourselves and get with it. Then we can just make peace with the fact that people in general just irritate us for no reason other than it's just other people.

The days of wine and roses have been replaced by the nights of brandy and dandelions. The winds of change are turning into a tornado of revolution, picking up Auntie Em's house and slamming it down in the middle of Pennsylvania Avenue. I'm not going to try to sway either side one way or another, but I will say this: the Trumpers have bullshitted themselves into believing that the only people who voted for HRC were the so-called coastal elites. They love their little map with the blue bits (higher populated areas) and the massive red parts (very misleading, seeing as they've filled in lower populated/unpopulated areas instead of leaving it gray). They've lied to themselves that the Cheeto has a "mandate," that more people voted for Trump than Clinton II. The thing is, though, not only did Clinton get 3 million more votes in the popular category, but when you factor in the people who voted for Johnson, Stein, and others, then include the people who didn't vote, you have a *lot* more people—*way* more people—who didn't vote for Trump. So Trumpers, I wouldn't get cocky. We outnumber you by nearly 10 million. If the time comes, if the shit hits the fan, there are way more of us than there are of you, and we have more conviction. Do not commit the cardinal sin of believing everything the Orange Leader tells you—even a halfway intelligent person knows that 98 percent of the shit he sends out there is fucking lies and bullshit.

One of these days this war will end. But first it has to begin, in earnest.

But what do I know? I'm an asshole, right?

CHAPTER 11

JOIN OR DIE

WHEN I WAS A KID I SAW THINGS VERY SIMPLY.

I have memories that are cascaded in orange speckles, with tiny dots of light, dancing around the brown in my hair and around my face and eyes. As an adult I know now that this was sunlight doing its best to shine through the hard polyester knit of the living room curtains in our old house in Clear Lake, Iowa, the dots merely dust particles refracting light and standing out against the dark brown of our old scratchy couch I used to call "Rowlf" because it looked like it was made from the same material as that crazy piano-playing dog from *The Muppets*. I used to kneel on Rowlf and look out the window on sunny days when I was too tired to go outside and play, and I would jump up and down to unleash the meteor shower of dust bits into the air so I could swat at them and make them go nuts, caught in the maelstrom of wind in my hand's wake. It's a vivid recollection I have—not attached to any one memory, mind you, but one that feels like a scene I relived over and over even as I remember it now, over and over. I guess the point is that I've always looked at things differently from how others see the world. Yes, I could distill and observe quietly and simply, but I could also unleash my imagination at a *very* young age, turning things as common and arbitrary as dust particles into celestial bodies of wonder. As I got old enough to appreciate this gift, it became harder and harder for me to relate my visions to other people. Maybe that's why I have tried so hard to make sure I still relate to people *in general.* When your brain has a tendency to drift and reconstruct, you have to maintain a tether to this world or else you'll be doomed to drift in and out of realms of fancy until even the ones you love become strangers in your mind's own movie.

That's how life is for me, even when talking about something as urbane and stepped on as this crazy fucking country called the United States of America. On the one hand, I love the challenge in taking all of this in: the purest form of buffoonery and boundless talent crashing together to form some sort of hyper-Greece, full of warriors, artists, and imbeciles all on the verge of greatness because in a democracy you can do and be anything you want as long as you obey the laws. Now some of those same crazies will fight you all day, making claims that this is not in fact a democracy. However, only in a democracy could someone come out and say some dumb shit like that. Boy, do we *ever* say some dumb-ass shit. We say so much dumb shit that we even find ourselves becoming accustomed to the cesspool of our egos, deciding all at once that every fucking idea we come up with is not only true if we can get enough people to agree with it but also cool on top of it all. Our idiotic forms of celebrity are living asshole proof of this statement.

I remember laughing like a hyena on meth when Kanye West married Kim Kardashian. It made so much sense: a bitchy, conceited, egotistical maniac . . . marrying a Kardashian. The sad thing is that if their fuck-knuckle fan base had started a petition to have their firstborn North West (jeeeeez . . .) declared a national treasure when he was born, I wouldn't have been the least bit surprised. That's because to a lot of Americans they are our new royalty. Maybe this is the whole reason I wanted to write this book in the first place: because we stopped appreciating talent and exceptional gifts and started worshipping a bunch of fucking glorified squatters. We went from JFK and Jackie O to reality TV ass clowns. We went from giving credit where credit is due to putting liens on the credit of the "star" because in at least one episode they get drunk and shit themselves on camera . . . *live.* No wonder ticket sales for zoo attendance seem to have plummeted. It's not the pro-animal protesters; it's because we have become the monkeys slinging shit at each other on TV. We are Harambe.

USA! USA! USA! USA . . .

That seems par for the course, really. Nothing in our country makes sense past the surface, the safety sniff. The argument could be made that idiocy and hypocrisy is as American as apple pie and Tennessee whiskey. I mean, it *has* to be—our very Constitution reflects that. To quote my patron saint George Carlin, "This country was founded by *slave owners* . . . who wanted to be *free.*" So how can the American Hypocrite not be right up there next to bald eagles and Uncle Sam? More importantly, why are we so gung-ho obstinate in the face of that kind of mirrored reality? Why haven't we embraced this two-faced image and stuck it on a flag of some kind? The answer is simple: because not only are we full of shit to each other, we're full of shit to ourselves. The Great Lie is that all Americans are noble, decent, hard-working, god-fearing people who will fight tyranny to the end and always do what's right for the greater good and democracy because the USA is truly the land of the free and the home of the brave.

Yeah . . . not so much.

Sometimes we can't even get our own lies straight. The double standards are endless. Look at this last election. The Republican Party has always purported to stand for the working man. It has always tried to be the blue-collar party, the family values party, the Christian party. The party of the every-man has a great bullshit story because I can't even remember the last time their party nominated an every-man. None of these motherfuckers come close, and neither do their policies. Donald Trump certainly doesn't. By the way, did you see him on Inauguration Day? I've never seen a person who just won the presidency look so fucking morose and depressed about it. Hold that thought—we'll get back to him in a minute.

Before I get off on the wrong foot here, let me tell you a story.

It was the summer of 1986. I was twelve on the verge of thirteen. The Bears won the Super Bowl, and the *Challenger* lost its crew live on TV. Coke Classic was the new thing, and I was making the journey from kid to dude with no one to give me a hand. The most exciting thing to happen to me that summer was a firecracker going off in my hand before I could throw it out the front door on the Fourth of July, and quite frankly that was the *best* thing to happen to me that summer. This was during the era when my mom, sister, and I were still living with her "best friend" Corky, a horrible, abusive, controlling, drug-addicted alcoholic with turquoise rings and something against little kids, especially ones who weren't her own. There was no escape and no real safety to be had, and I took a giant share of it. So when Rick, Corky's boyfriend at the time, asked me if I wanted to ride cross-country in a semi delivering goods for the company he worked for, I said yes—even though I didn't really want to go. He wasn't much of a prize either—our house was reality TV without the cameras, with shit-tons of violence, domestic and foreign. It was *Cops* on the worst night ever. But anything that would get me out of that house was welcome, at least for a little while. So we set off from our old house off of Lafayette Road in Elk Run Heights, Iowa, heading west for Billings, Montana. Rick was up front with his dad, whose name I didn't care enough to remember. I was tucked back in the "driver's nook," the bed where the driver sleeps when he pulls over for a few minutes of shut-eye—you know, usually when the crank wears off.

Now let me explain to you what an exceptionally creepy place a driver's nook can be.

I laid back there pretty much exclusively because there was no room up front and also because I didn't really give a soggy shit about the conversation that was going on up there to begin with. It was almost always about drinking, fucking, trying to drink while fucking, trying to fuck while *drinking*, what a bitch my mom was, what a bitch Corky was (I could certainly agree with that), hunting, fishing, country music, and, most importantly, how many beers you could drink before it was someone else's turn to drive. Every once in a while they'd toss a question over their shoulders at me in an attempt to include me in their shit-talk. "So Corey, ever been huntin'?" No. "No?!" No.

Silence . . .

Riveting.

So mainly I turned my attention to unearthing shit in the nook. I'll be honest: the stuff I found back there was pretty fucked-up shit for a preteen to discover. Condoms, porno mags, whiskey bottles, cigarette packs, and so on. Remember: this was the eighties. Nobody was regulating decency yet. It was the Wild

West in silver and neon pink. So I learned what a whiskey hangover felt like, I smoked behind their backs, and I basked in the knowledge that (a) Ginger Lynn was a porn star, and (b) Ginger Lynn had just released a "very realistic sex doll." This was important information for a formative mind like mine. It was going to be a looooooooong ride. Mainly I just slept and tried to keep the cigarette ash out of my eyes and hair when it would blow back on me from their windows up front. Those fuckers could *smoke*—they made me look like an amateur.

This all culminated in the night we almost died.

We'd stopped on the side of the road to relieve our bladders—the nearest rest area wasn't for miles, and between the two of them, Rick and his father had polished off at *least* a case of PBR. (That would be Pabst Blue Ribbon for anyone who's not a redneck, a hipster . . . or any person who's not dead, I guess—why the hell am I telling you what PBR means? I'm sure you know this!) So we parked next to a field not too far from the interstate, spread out, and commenced to go find some quiet patch to drain our respective lizards. I finished first, so I was heading back toward the semi when I heard a different semi's horn blaring in the distance. That's when I saw what was about to happen to us.

Picture this: I was about one hundred yards from the semi (I like privacy when I'm pissing in public), but I could see the highway clearly laid out in front of me. About half a mile down the road another semi was *screaming* toward our semi . . . and I mean HAULING TONS OF ASS TOWARD OUR SEMI. The angle I was looking at it, it was going to crush our truck. I started yelling for Rick because something bad was about to happen, and that's when I saw his dad busting ass across the field to get to the truck so he could move it. For some reason the other truck wasn't even *trying* to slow down—it was shooting toward us at an alarming rate. I caught up to Rick as we were trying to get to the truck in time. His dad was already up in the cabin—we heard the engine firing up. The truck was almost on top of us. That's when it hit me: if the semi hit ours, it was going to be *bad*. Rick's dad would surely die, and as Rick and I got closer, our radius to the damage would ensure we were dead too. I didn't know what to do—I felt like I should stop running, but I also knew I should keep going. I wasn't sure what the hell I thought I was going to do to help—I couldn't drive a *regular* manual transmission, let alone a fucking semi—but I kept going anyway.

Thank Christ Rick's dad knew what to do. With a sure hand and steadiness under pressure, he fired up the truck, moving it further off the road and farther down the highway just in time. The renegade semi merely clipped the driver side rearview mirror and scraped a bunch of paint from the trailer and cab. Rick and I had to run/walk a bit to find the truck, but that was better than blowing up in the middle of nowhere. Come to find out that the other truck's brakes had failed and the driver was trying to downshift to slow it down when he'd come upon our truck. Nobody was hurt, but it could've been *so* bad for everyone involved.

We fished our way through Middle America, through North Platte and other places I tried like hell to find something to do in, until we finally made it to Billings, Montana, where we ended up staying at a place called the Yellow Rose Ranch for a while. You guys may remember me talking about this place in my first book. I'll give you a little more detail. It was a nice little spread just outside of Billings, with four out-buildings, a long winding dirt road for the cattle, and the main house, which sat assed up against a hillside covered in trees. Sure, it was just a doublewide trailer, but seeing as all the houses I'd ever lived in had never been my own nor very majestic, it was like something out of a Louis L'Amour book.

Rick and his dad were too busy working or doing god knows fuck to entertain a gnarly kid with a dozen years under his belt, and seeing as there were no other kids there, I was alone a lot. So I figured some shit out on my own. I chopped down some trees in the forests behind the main house. I dug a swamp with a shovel and filled it with well water, convinced I could "lure frogs to my waters." (I was a fucking weird kid.) And the one thing I did that I will never forget is I taught myself how to drive in an eighties Toyota truck with no siding, only two working gears and a roll cage designed not to save *your* life but really just to keep the cattle out. This thing was a *glorious* piece of shit—even the pipes that made up the cage and frame were different colors. I wasn't exactly supposed to drive the thing, but seeing as I was the only fucker around to do anything, I decided it was worth the ass whooping. I got really good at it, which is fortunate because even though I couldn't afford to get my license for *years*, I could drive anything you put in front of me.

This is usually the part in my books where you, the reader, are naturally thinking, *Well, this reads like typical Taylor: he cuts a swath through the prior pages just to get to some tale from when he was growing up that is* clearly *a metaphor for whatever tone or moral he wants to foist on us, whether we like it or not.* Yep. Pretty much. Even as I scoff at your pretentious snarcasm, I will give you this: you read me like a book. But allow me to retort: this *is* a book, dipshit. I know I tend to go off on tangents and whatnot, but I hope you know I always have a point. I do. I do have a point. I'd better have a point; I'm wearing my Pantaloons of Eternal Wisdom, and they were on *sale*. Shit, where was I . . .

So . . . what have we learned? Hmm?

Jesus, I can *feel* your lawsuits heating up.

I'm not a subtle person—I am blunt-force trauma in ill-fitting jeans. So if this book has offended you, it's *your* fault. I've never made any bones about who I am or what I believe, and if this book caught you off guard, I don't care. I wear my empathy on my sleeve, but don't think for a second I won't roll these sleeves up to get my hands dirty. Besides, I think you're *all* fucked in the head. Between your weekly protests and your nightly news, my migraines have now registered to vote just to find the quiet candidates.

All you motherfuckers who think this country would be better if it went back to the "good old days," you should probably understand something. Back then fear dictated that certain people of color wouldn't fight back because they were afraid of "The Swarm." The Swarm was basically so many racists coming all at once that there was nowhere to run and no way to fight back. I've seen the footage, which, it pains me to say, includes police officers from back in the day. In the "good old days" you could get away with literal murder. You could use your station in life to lord over others just to make yourself feel better about nothing at all. The "good old days" were only good for a handful. Those days, thankfully, are dead. Done. Fucking. Over. This generation has grown up in an era when not only have they been encouraged to fight back, but also now truly *anyone*—including them—could be elected president of the United States of America. So all you motherfuckers pining and crying for the "good old days," you'd better listen up right now. Your shitty scare tactics may have worked in the past, but they're not going to work anymore. This generation and all its beautiful colors are ready to fight for the ground they've gained, they've earned, and they've fought for.

What's more, there are literally *millions* of people like me who will be right there ready to help as well. So if you think you're going to "do your worst," be prepared to deal with this country's best. There are *way* more of us than there are of you. I'm going to go out on a limb here and say that back in the "good old days," math was not a strong suit for you dicks. Let's put it on paper: the Hillary voters, plus Stein voters, plus Johnson voters, plus the undecideds who didn't vote but are now pissed off, plus the ones who *did* vote for the Cheeto but are now starting to see that he wasn't going to keep any of the real promises he made—that's a massive fuck-off number. You know what that means? There are way more of us than there are of you. And not one of us is afraid of you.

Watch what happens when your hate meets our resistance.

I don't want this book to end on a shit note. Too many of our stories tend to be destined for the flush these days. Yes, I'm fucking repelled and angry about the state of the Greatest Country in the World (patent pending), but I also still love and hold dear some of the things that matter, even if only from a cerebral standpoint. I love that you can still go from coast to coast unchallenged in search of adventure, yourself, or just looking for a new home. I love that even in bigger cities, family is still something that is cherished and regarded with a sense of pride and protection. I love that you can still get into good, old-fashioned trouble in places like New Orleans, New York City, Miami, Los Angeles, or a thousand other places here. Yes, there are dangers, but if you live your life stuck in the loop of irrational fear, you'll *never* have a reason to be afraid in the first place: look at the sad example your life has become when you're so busy worrying about the loss of it that you forget to loosen up and fucking *live it.* That's what fear mongers do: they goose that gland in your head that keeps you in a state of constant neuroses and puts you on the edge of absolute anxiety all to get you running back for the voting booth so they can keep controlling you with that fear. Fuck that. FUCK THAT, GOD DAMNIT! This is America. We're not meant to live under control to deal with fear. We're meant to control our fear to show motherfuckers what the deal is. And the deal is this: YOU'RE NEVER GOING TO BEAT US. YOU'RE NEVER GOING TO HURT US. YOU KNOCK US DOWN? WE WILL JUST CLIMB BACK TO OUR FEET, COME OFF THE WALL, AND GO DOWN FIGHTING IF NEED BE. To quote Captain America (you're fucking right I'm going to quote Captain America): "I can do this all day."

Ultimately, though, at some point, if we want this country to get on better footing, we need to find some common fucking ground. These days that seems like a tall order, seeing as both sides of the political aisle find it easier to attack each other than talk *to* each other, like smashing two fists together in an attempt to lace your fingers. Anyone watching these days is probably scared shitless; we're all surrounded by fascists in sheep's clothing, except one group is in fifty-fifty polycotton, and the other is in all-natural biodegradable diesel textiles. All they want is for you to support their cause, no matter where it takes you in the end, but if you deign to disagree—even if it's just a matter of opinion and it's not a big detail to get hung up on—they'll vilify you in the town square, screaming "NAZI" or "FAKE NEWS" or "SNOWFLAKE" or "DEPLORABLE" or a zillion other fucking catchphrases the media has pushed on the public for no reason other than to appear relevant in an age when print feels dead, news feels forced, and if information doesn't come fast enough, it gets fucking made up. Sound familiar? Feel like shit? I couldn't agree more.

On your way out the door, let me tell you about the Murder Hotel.

Before you start thinking crazy thoughts or if you're wondering whether I'm going to pitch you on one of my shitty scripts (I'm telling you, *Cul-De-Slash* is going to be a *hit!*), I promise you it's a true story, no one gets murdered, and it has a happy ending. It's meant to be a metaphor, just like the story about Rick and his dad a few pages back. I know I didn't exactly tell you what the metaphor was when I told you that story, so maybe by kicking this tale down the drain as well I'll be able to kill two birds with one stone, so to speak. I *do* have a point to make, I just can't remember which bubble I wanted to burst with said point, so I need to find my way back to it by going over this story with you all. Come on, have I *ever* let you down before? What? What was the *second* time? I only remember the one with the goose and the Mason jar, and that was *hardly* my fucking fault, seeing as I wasn't the one who made the dare in the first place! I *knew* that damn bird wouldn't make the distance, so don't blame me! Shit got everywhere, ruined my good venetian blinds, and I lost twenty fucking bucks. NO ONE WON THAT DAY, YOU CALLOUS DICKS.

It's happening again, I know . . .

Anyway, my son Griff and I went on a road trip of our own.

My family has houses in Iowa and Nevada. A few years ago we decided to switch cars, from Iowa to Nevada. So my son Griff and I loaded ourselves in for a cross-country trek. Well, I guess it would be a half-cross-country trek—what's half of a country? Maybe half of the word country . . . rhymes with "front" . . . I'm drawing a blank right now. . . . Anyway, we logged the coordinates in the good ol' GPS system and proceeded to the highlighted route just in time to catch some killer shit on the eighties on eight. Griff, brutal typical teenager that he is, simply rolled his eyes at my choice of songs (he's finally come around to appreciating "good musical nostalgia") and sank into the backseat for the first of many naps on our trip. I settled down on my sit bones, getting both cheeks on the same page, and allowed my journey to roll out in front of me. Unlike most people, I absolutely adore road trips. Maybe it's because I basically grew up on the road. Maybe it's because of the stories like the Semi Near-Death one with Rick and his dad. Maybe it's because the more I drive through this country, the more connected I feel to it, like following the veins and arteries that keep our nation running. Maybe it's the hypnotic swing that comes with staring at the white and yellow lines for too long. Hell, it could be as simple as road trips are the best times to listen to good music. Whatever the reason, I've always loved to be on the pavement, racing toward a faraway destination. Something about it just feels like freedom. That may sound corny, but to me it's the purest form I can think of right now.

Anyway, off we sped on our day-and-a-half trip. We were making fairly decent time considering how late we left, but by the time we reached Denver it was about time to stop for the night. I made a quick decision not to stop and find a hotel in Denver itself because I wouldn't want to deal with the traffic once we hit the road again in the morning. So we drove on through the city, opting for a smaller hotel on the other side closer to the mountains. Not only was this a fucking stupid thing to do, but it also turned out to be a fateful idea because we weren't quite prepared for the ridiculousness waiting to unfold out in front of us in the darkness. After maneuvering through the late-night traffic, we motored on out of town, looking for those exits of promise: hotel, restaurant, and gas, like little islands of civilization among the rocks of desolation, the boondocks of the greater Denver area. We found the exit we were looking for—a nice-sized Best Western with the lights on, right next to a gas station so we could fuel up in the morning. So we stopped, pulled up, parked, and stretched some blood into our legs as we walked inside. The nice man behind the counter gave us two very troubling words.

"No vacancy."

Ah . . .

Well, shit.

But that made sense. It *was* after midnight, and these parts tended to cater to tourists, so of course they were going to be booked up for the night. But there was no need to panic—that very rationale meant that there were other hotels out there in the darkened distance, just waiting for a couple of road-weary travelers. Unfortunately we ran into the same reaction at the next hotel as well. I was worried for a second—the sign I'd just passed said there wasn't anything for another forty miles. I didn't want to drive all night just to get to a hotel for a nap; I needed some fucking sleep. Griff, now *wide awake* because of his twenty-five teenage naps during the drive, was suddenly interested in what was going on. I assured him we'd be okay as I turned down the final exit before the drive got a little longer than I'd hoped for the night. This one looked promising: there were several signs for hotels down the two-lane run, so we passed the first hotel off the exit—just across from a McDonald's—and headed down the street. The good news was that there were indeed a shitton of hotels to choose from. The bad news was that every god damn one of them was closed. I couldn't understand it: the office doors were unlocked and I could see people milling about in their rooms and out to the ice machine and whatever. But there was no manager on duty, and no one answered the bells when I'd ring them. This happened at four different places—the rest of the fucking hotels had their lights off. I was dumbfounded. I'd never seen anything like it. We reached the end of the ironic "hotel row" and were forced to turn around. Griff said, "Well, *now* what do we do?" As we reached the highway where we pulled off, I told him not to worry, that we'd find something eventually. That's when I realized we'd passed the first hotel by the Mickey D's without even checking to see if it had rooms for the night. So with a quiet hope I pulled in and went inside.

The front desk was empty, but this time when I rang the bell a very nice old Vietnamese man came out and asked me if I needed a room. With a sigh of relief, I said yes and we began the paperwork. Out the window I gave Griff the "A-okay" sign. Once I'd settled the bill, he handed me the key, and this was the first sign that things weren't going to be your standard J/11 evening out and about. The key was straight out of the 1970s: hard metal like a house key, hanging from a big diamond-shaped keychain, on which was a numbered sticker delineating the room number: 16. For a second I was kind of amazed at the "old-school analog" feel of the thing in my hand. It never occurred to me that this *may* be a warning sign. I just shrugged, giggled, went out, and got in the car, handing the key to Griff ("What the hell is *this*?" he said). We pulled around the back of the hotel to where our "room" was located. We rolled past what I can only describe as dark cement cinder-block outbuildings designed to be used as laundry facilities in most major trailer parks, until we reached number 16. We parked directly across from it, grabbed our gear, and with a deft turn of the key in the lock . . . the door wouldn't open. So I tried again—no bueno. Finally, after frantically jiggling the handle as hard as I could, the antiquated locking mechanism eventually gave in, and the handle from the past turned. I said to myself, *Jesus Christ, okay, settle down. Time to relax*. I opened the door, and my son and I were immediately assaulted by the most horrible stench I had experienced in a very long time. It smelled like a dead hooker had been raped by another dead hooker while they were both drenched in cat piss.

We both stood at the door, reeling from the lambasting we'd just taken from the ferocious odor, neither of us in any real hurry to go inside. It was *that* fucking bad. For a second I felt like we should call the authorities for fear that we were walking into a crime scene. But once I turned on the lights there were no obvious signs that anything nefarious had been committed. So I went in first, just to make sure myself. Griff followed after a moment, looking nervous and leery about getting comfortable in a place that we may have need to flee at a moment's notice. It might have been the oddest hotel room I've ever set foot in: everything about it was wrong. There were two beds, like I'd asked for, but they were set up perpendicular to each other, at strange angles that didn't make any sense. The TV was in the corner—an old thirty-five-inch tube TV from the early nineties (ironically with *full* DirecTV access). The bathroom was against the far wall, opening up like a long closet. Between the mold growing in the shower and what looked like a false wall made of paneling, I decided neither of us would be using those facilities very much. The paneling wall is also why we christened it "The Murder Hotel"—all night long I had visions of that sliding open to reveal the killer, stalking his prey H. H. Holmes style and using our meat in some crazy form of Sweeney Todd room service. Before you ask, yes, I *do* watch the Investigation Discovery Channel—why?

We stood pondering the bathroom for several minutes, as I took pictures to send to The Boss in a "you're never gonna believe this" sort of way. We were still holding our bags like we were afraid to put them on the floor, just in case our backpacks contracted carpet chlamydia. As I FaceTimed the family back home to show them what kind of situation we were dealing with, I swung the camera around to the radiator, placed just to the right of the door. Suddenly I realized there was something sitting on it. At first I couldn't really believe what I was seeing. I mean, it was so out of place that I didn't want to trust what my eyes were making me have to deal with at that moment. After the absolute assholing we'd already taken at the hands of this bastard room, you'd think I would've just nodded and been like, "Yep, makes total fucking sense." But no. I balked so hard at the absurdity that the reality took a second to catch up to me, like an echo down a long valley. I blinked, asked Griff to confirm what I was seeing, and then offered a glimpse to the people on the other end of the phone.

Resting on the radiator, as if it'd been abandoned in an earthquake evacuation, was a fucking gross grungy toilet brush.

It seriously looked like someone had taken a call while they were cleaning the bathroom, put it down as they walked outside to talk, and had simply forgotten it was there, never coming back to retrieve it. I was baffled. I didn't want to touch it, and I wouldn't let Griff fuck with it—we both just tried to ignore it. Weirdly, Griff slept like a fucking champ, whereas I spent all night thinking there were bedbugs in my hair. As *soon* as the sun came up, I had him up and ready to go. I was smoking at the time, so as I stepped out to have a cigarette, I noticed a man doing the exact same thing. We made eye contact, and he said, "Your room smell as bad as ours did?" When I said yes he told me that he'd been through there a few months prior and the whole place had been underwater. So basically we'd all been breathing mold all night. That was pretty kick-asteroid. It took two Starbucks Americanos and driving with the window down for a few hours to make me feel like I didn't have fucking black lung. Griff loves that fucking story—makes me tell it to this day. Unfortunately, every time I think about the experience, I break out in fucking hives.

Here's the point of that story—and the Semi Near-Death story as well, as I blew right by it earlier. I make no qualms about the fact that I'm a pretty progressive dude. In fact, I am of two minds: to steal a quote from my good friend Stubs, I am socially liberal yet fiscally conservative. I've talked about why I subscribe to both ways of thinking, and I've always maintained that most people are like this, regardless of what the professional politicians try to force down our throats. But I'm also open enough to say that I can find common ground with people who may or may not believe the things I believe or subscribe to the values and ideas that I hold. I don't expect everyone to feel the same way I do on things—we're all different, and expecting everyone to blindly accept the various things thrown at them is fucking idiotic and naïve. Yet that's not to say we couldn't get there *some*day. Just giving up socially is fucking pathetic as well. That's why my feet are planted *firmly* in the center, away from all the extreme shit and cancerous garbage they use to keep us at each other's throats. No matter what I've said in this book and no matter what you think about me and my opinion, please understand something: I am first and foremost an American who loves his country and his people. I worry about everyone who was born here and everyone who fought like heroes to get here and everyone who dreamed and managed to stay here. I don't mean to offend my white American brothers and sisters; however, looking American doesn't mean looking whiter. Being American means just that: THERE ARE NO RIGHT WAYS TO LOOK FUCKING AMERICAN, no matter what those assholes who stir up shit try to say.

One of the things I love about this country is that we are *always* moving forward. From the minute we were conceived as a theocratic idea, we were designed to evolve, constantly evolve, to the point where our documents are living documents and our nation is a living nation. We were set up to live in the future, not die in the past. It's the thing that separates us the most from the older republics. When we talk about freedom for all, it's not meant to be about freedom for a certain group of people at a certain period in our history; it's about working our way through the stereotypes and prejudices, looking for the common ground to guarantee that promise Thomas Jefferson first wrote and then Abraham Lincoln paraphrased: ALL MEN (AND WOMEN) ARE CREATED EQUAL. Of course, I added that little bit about women because it's not in the original document. Granted, most great minds are hindered by the class and gender biases of their eras; however, that doesn't mean we should detract from the *message*; it simply means we should stand on their shoulders to reach the light.

On a clear day, when the storms have stopped blowing us over or raining on our parades, we'll look up from our bunkers or we'll peek out from behind our walls and realize the war is over, the sun is shining, and maybe, for the first time in forever, we'll be able to find a way to come to terms with everything that has been swirling around our heads. There will be no more AM blasts on Twitter, no more resignations amidst perjury or other illegal acts, no more sitting at the right hand of ignorance, and no more choosing insanity over rationality. Much like when the Germans and the Allies stepped out onto No Man's Land that Christmas Day during World War I, we will be able to put aside so many differences and *listen*, really listen, because we won't feel so far away that we come off as misunderstood and, by that mindset, not so misunderstood that we have to scream at each other. Maybe the message is in the nuance. Maybe the malice comes from the measures we take just to be right. I may be wrong. But I don't think I am.

Years ago I started this book with one intention: to point out the absurdities that make our country sort of a fundamental funhouse. Later it became something a little more self-righteous: deciding what was better for people after a millionaire tyrant was "defeated" in the name of democracy and the right thing to do. Not too long ago, after a decent dish of "should've kept my fucking mouth shut," it became something simpler, something better and more substantial: a possibility to get everyone to come together and be a country again instead of a collection of regions bent on surviving change. Have I pulled it off? Fuck, I don't know. But at least I gave it a shot. So many people are so concerned with pulling up "stats" and "facts" that they refuse to see where the problem was in the first place: that they didn't listen to begin with.

When the time comes, when the hammer falls, when the light reveals what we've all feared all along, will we all be willing to accept what is right in front of us? Will we be ready to stand together because it's the right thing to do? Can we set aside our falsehoods to build our brother and sisterhood again? I hope so. The last time our nation was this split, thousands died—but millions were freed. There must be a silver lining in this somewhere beyond the pale quality of our own stubbornness. Tomorrows will happen with or without us; it all comes down to whether we all would like to wake up together and feel the same sort of sun on our faces. There will always be disagreements, but there doesn't always need to be contention. I believe that when the chips are down, we'll all flop in as a team, ready to win it all and split the spoils, basking in the glory that is pure and unadulterated freedom and prosperity. And why not? That's a "happily ever after" I can gladly live with.

After all, isn't that the American way?

ACKNOWLEDGMENTS

This book took a lot out of me, so I'm blessed to be surrounded by people who helped me do it: My wife Stephanie; my editor and friend Ben Schafer; my agent and friend Marc Gerald; my family at 5B: Cory Brennan, Bob Johnson, Kim Schon, Brad Furman, Harold Gutierrez, Brit Buckley, and any I might've missed; my massive family: the Taylors, the Bonnicis, the Mays, the Williams, the Bennetts, the Ballards . . . my artistic conspirator, P. R. Brown; my cast of '51': Roy Mayorga, Jason Christopher, Kira Kawakami, James Ingram, Art Ruffin, Brittany Curran, Debi Kohos, and Harold as "Uncle Santos"; and of course, all my fans. I love you and cherish you. See you out there, somewhere . . .